brilliant

how to influence in any situation

brilliant

how to
influence
in any
situation

Mike Clayton

PEARSON

Harlow, England • London • New York • Boston • San Francisco • Toronto • Sydney • Auckland • Singapore • Hong Kong
Tokyo • Seoul • Taipei • New Delhi • Cape Town • São Paulo • Mexico City • Madrid • Amsterdam • Munich • Paris • Milan

PEARSON EDUCATION LIMITED

Edinburgh Gate
Harlow CM20 2JE
United Kingdom
Tel: +44 (0)1279 623623
Web: www.pearson.com/uk

First published in Great Britain as *Brilliant Influence* 2011 (print)
Rejacketed edition published 2015 (print and electronic)

© Pearson Education 2011 (print)
© Pearson Education 2015 (print and electronic)

The right of Mike Clayton to be identified as author of this work has been
asserted by him in accordance with the Copyright, Designs and Patents Act 1988.

Pearson Education is not responsible for the content of third-party internet sites.

ISBN: 978-1-292-08327-8 (print)
       978-1-292-08403-9 (PDF)
       978-1-292-08402-2 (ePub)
       978-1-292-08401-5 (eText)

British Library Cataloguing-in-Publication Data
A catalogue record for the print edition is available from the British Library

Library of Congress Cataloging-in-Publication Data
A catalog record for the print edition is available from the Library of Congress

10 9 8 7 6 5 4 3 2
19 18 17 16

Series cover design by David Carroll & Co
Print edition typeset in 10/14pt Plantin MT Pro by 71
Print edition printed and bound in Great Britain by Henry Ling Limited,
at the Dorset Press, Dorchester DT1 1HD

NOTE THAT ANY PAGE CROSS REFERENCES REFER TO THE PRINT EDITION

This book is dedicated to my father, Gerald Clayton. He would have been proud to read it but sadly died just as the first draft was finished, and never had the chance. Re-reading the material on integrity, optimism and resilience, I realised how much I learned from him, and how much I will miss him.

Contents

About the author

Mike Clayton started working life in the academic world and has since been a consultant and project manager, a trainer and executive coach, and a facilitator and speaker. Throughout this time he has observed some of the most influential people and how they are able to influence the people around them. Over the last 20 years he has studied the science of influence and honed his skills, while starting two successful businesses and becoming a respected public speaker and author. Over the last eight years Mike has trained and spoken extensively on the subject of influence and persuasion, helping people to articulate their message persuasively and put it across in a compelling and powerful way.

Mike has a science PhD from the University of Manchester and is an NLP Master Practitioner. As a volunteer, he has been a Chair of Governors and a trustee of two charities.

Acknowledgements

I would like to acknowledge the astonishing support I have had from my wife, Felicity, throughout the writing process. I never seem to thank you enough for your belief in me and for the time you have given me this year, to pursue my dream. Thank you again.

There have been so many people who have influenced me over my life, and so taught me about influence. I can only single out a few, very special influences: Emma Francis, Simon Danciger, Dr John Shepherd, Professor Henry Hall, Rob Francis, Chris Sullivan, Gilbert Toppin, Rex Mackrill, Brian Green, Judith Wilks, John Everett, Sir John Whitmore and Julian Badcock. I wish I were still in touch with all of you.

I would like to thank my editor, Samantha Jackson.

Finally, most of all, I would like to thank my parents for all the opportunities and support they gave me. I am just sorry this book did not come two years earlier, when they could both have enjoyed it.

Introduction

Influence is one of the most powerful skills around. It allows us instantly to earn the trust and respect of others, and lead and manage teams, individuals and situations with power, confidence and success. Most crucially, it enables us to make things happen in all aspects of our lives. The positive effects of influence are far-reaching yet no one ever teaches us how to develop this essential life and work skill.

How to Influence in Any Situation has been written to change all this. I have spent the past 20 years analysing the behaviour of skilled communicators and influencers in commercial, political and voluntary arenas. I have worked with many inspirational teachers and researched the scientific literature to bring you a step-by-step, practical guide to influence.

Influence is all about how you can affect other people's attitudes and behaviour. We do this by the way we communicate – both consciously and unconsciously. *How to Influence in Any Situation* will show you how to influence colleagues, business contacts, friends and family, by honing the unconscious messages you send out, improving your conscious communication skills, and creating powerful, compelling messages that appeal to people's psychological needs and desires.

The three components of influence

The amount of influence you have depends on three things: you (your confidence and presence), your message (how you craft a speech, a conversation, a presentation), and the way you deliver your message (how you negotiate and persuade). To master the art of influence you need to be strong in each area and *How to Influence in Any Situation* shows you how to do just that.

Part 1 focuses on the first of these three components – you and your role in the influencing process. I will start with the fundamental components of influence and move on to look at specific areas such as body language and how to use other people's decision-making styles to influence their choices. I will end the section by studying how a range of psychological insights can enhance your effectiveness as an influencer.

Part 2 looks at your message. Both what you say and how you say it are equally important in the influencing process, so we will explore both. In Chapter 5 we will examine how you can put a structured and compelling message together; and, in Chapter 6, you will learn how you can use your language to inspire and engage your listeners.

Part 3 will help you to make the most out of your message and develop your own personal influencing style. You will learn how to negotiate and balance your interests with others, how to build a network of influence, and how to put together all the tools and techniques in this book to handle common influencing challenges.

To become a brilliant influencer takes time and practice. I am certain that, if you master each of the three components of influence, you will become a better influencer and, eventually, become capable of Brilliant Influence.

PART 1

Fundamentals

CHAPTER 1

Use your common sense: the basics of influence

We are all born with influencing skills. Babies can get attention when they need it and toddlers are even more influential, using charm and tantrums to get what they want.

As we grow older, we add more layers to these innate influencing skills, introducing such things as persuasion and flirtation. Most of us are unaware that we are doing this – it comes naturally. Our education teaches us to use another powerful influencing skill: reason. So, already, whether you know it or not, you have some finely honed influencing skills that you can work with.

In this chapter I want to focus on your innate influencing skills and show you how you can use them to create a strong base for the brilliant influencing skills that will follow.

The four things we all know about influence

By the time we leave school, we have learned four fundamental things about how to influence the people around us: the "four As of influence".

- *Actions.* "Actions speak louder than words" is a cliché because it is true. We will look at what three actions speak loudest and have the greatest positive impact on other people.

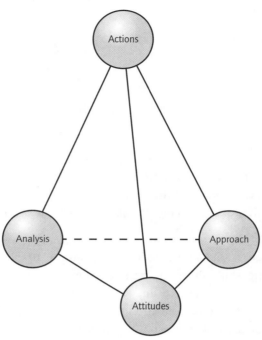

Figure 1.1 The four As of influence

- *Attitudes.* Our attitudes infect the people around us. I will show you the three brilliant attitudes that send powerful messages about who you are and why people should be influenced by you.

- *Analysis.* Being able to give compelling reasons is a crucial part of being influential. I will show you how to prepare for influence and a great technique for overcoming resistance when you disagree with someone.

- *Approach.* Early in life, we discover the three approaches that we can take to get what we want from other people. I call these "the good, the bad, and the ugly". In the last section of this chapter, I will offer you the choice.

Actions

 We need to be the change we wish to see in the world.

Mohandas K. Gandhi

Three types of action consistently impress others and encourage them to like, trust and respect you: courtesy, generosity and follow-through. Let's look at these one at a time.

Courtesy

Courtesy is a label for all those actions that both conform to social norms and make other people feel that it is a pleasure to be around you. Examples include letting people go first, holding doors, helping with parcels, and saying "thank you". These are not difficult, but they say a lot about you. They also trigger one of the most important influence responses, reciprocity: I am grateful for what you have done for me, so I want to do something in return.

Think about some times when you did people favours; did they thank you for it? An unacknowledged favour probably left you wondering why you bothered; but on another occasion, when you received proper thanks, you were probably pleased to have been of help. Maybe you have noticed that, while a general thank you is courteous, it has little impact, because it feels like a reflexive response. You can create more impact by making your "thank you" more specific. Try saying: "Thank you for ...".

Generosity

Generosity builds your influence in so many ways: showing you have the resources to be generous, creating a sense of reciprocal obligation, and showing you are thoughtful, for example.

Sharing ideas, donating your time, and not quibbling about details of who owes what to whom, are all indicators of generosity: they say, "here is someone of substance".

To build your influence, look for opportunities to be generous. Try thinking about your current colleagues and business contacts, and make a list of all of them down the left-hand side of a sheet of paper. Against each name, note down one generous thing you could do for that person in the next month.

Follow-through

When you make a commitment, see that you honour it. If you are unsure whether you will be able to, it is far better to not make the commitment in the first place. This way, you will get a reputation as someone who can be trusted and relied upon, which is important, because people will be attracted to you when your actions accord with your words.

brilliant tip

Keep a list of the commitments you make in your notebook, diary or organiser. Make sure you record the deadlines too, and schedule time to act on each undertaking. Best of all, if you use an electronic organiser, set a reminder.

Attitudes

The attitude you portray to the world says something important about who you really are. Your attitude will affect my behaviour and my attitude. Brilliant attitudes are self-reinforcing, as are negative attitudes. Three brilliant attitudes are: flexibility, persistence and optimism. Together, they will make you more resilient and able to cope with adversity, to take setbacks as challenges, and to keep going when you'd really rather curl up some-where cosy. Resilience is influential because it shows that you can stick with what you believe, and it demonstrates confidence and mental

> three brilliant attitudes are: flexibility, persistence and optimism

toughness. These are attractive character traits that we associate with influential people.

Flexibility

If two people are in the same situation and they want the same thing, then the one who is more flexible in their behaviour will get what they want; and the one who is more flexible in how they deal with the other will feel that they are in control. When we are willing to try different approaches, we often achieve our goals.

Do you remember a time when you tried to influence somebody and it was just not working? What did you do? If you ultimately failed, it is probably because you stuck to one or two ways of influencing them. If you succeeded, it may well have been because you switched tactics until you got the result you wanted. If at first you don't succeed; try something *different*!

Persistence

Persistence – although not to the point of futility – is an attractive attitude that also helps you to reach your goal. If you find someone is resistant to an offer or a request, then keep asking, but look for different ways to do so. People tend to agree to things after you have asked several times. Once or twice may not be enough; you may need to ask six or seven times. As long as you stay polite and are prepared to respect a clear request to stop, you have nothing to lose.

When have you recently tried to influence a situation and, looking back, you can see that you may have given in too soon? Maybe you still have a chance to go back and try again.

Optimism

An optimistic outlook is a huge asset. This is not about blindly believing that things will work out: it is about looking for opportunities that will move you towards the outcome you have planned.

A part of your brain called the reticular activating system (RAS) increases your alertness when it receives a relevant stimulus. If you know what you want, then your RAS will alert you to things in your environment that will help you achieve it. It is your RAS that is responsible for spotting lots of cars just like yours, whenever you change your car, and is often what helps you notice opportunities at just the right time, so I call it our "serendipity organ". Thanks to this fabulous piece of brain circuitry, optimism really can help you to get what you want.

Analysis

Humans are rational creatures and we need a reason to act. By analysing a situation accurately and presenting your conclusions logically, you will be more influential.

Preparation is all-important, because most of us are unable to develop an accurate rationale and a powerful influencing strategy on the spur of the moment. The more important something is, the more preparation it deserves. Yet, too often, people go into situations that really matter, without giving any thought to what outcome they want, and how to get it. As they say in the British Army, "Prior planning and preparation prevents pitifully poor performance."

Before you set out to influence anyone, in any context, the following process will help you to prepare.

1 Determine what you want to achieve.

2 Gather the facts.

3   Consider everyone's perceptions.

4   Decide how to approach the situation.

5   Identify what can go wrong and how you can handle it.

▶ **brilliant** example

Don't argue: cut-up pie

One of the worst things you can do if you want to influence someone is to allow yourself to get into an argument. When you imply someone is wrong, it activates their "reactance". This is the pressure we feel to act against a perceived force. If anything, arguing cements, rather than loosens, opinions.

Instead, look for opportunities to agree on a part of what you may otherwise argue about; it is easier to move from agreement to agreement than from disagreement to agreement. Then look at the remaining part which you disagree about. It is smaller, so not only do you now have some common ground, but the scope of your disagreement is smaller. Can you now further divide the area of disagreement into one part you agree on and one you don't?

If you can keep going like this, you'll find very little at issue, and your influencing task far easier. Here is an example of a dialogue that uses this technique. It starts with a challenge to a piece of work you have done:

Abe: "Your conclusions are all wrong; this piece of work is rubbish."

Bea: "You don't agree with my conclusions: is it the findings you disagree with or the way I interpreted them?"

Abe: "The findings are fine. Your analysis is wrong."

Bea: "OK, so we're agreed on the findings. Now, you don't like my analysis: is it my methodology you disagree with, or the way I carried it out?"

Abe: "You worked through it fine, but you should never have taken that approach."

Bea: "Good, so let's discuss what other approaches I could take."

Notice how you are both in agreement on a couple of issues and the scope of your disagreement is now much narrower (as shown in the diagram). You are no longer going to argue about whether the work is rubbish; instead, you can discuss approaches in a rational way.

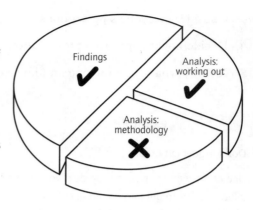

Approach

The influencing skills in this book are powerful. So how you use them is important, if you want to build sustained influence, and feel good about yourself. There are three approaches you can take, which I call "the good, the bad and the ugly" – these are, respectively: integrity, coercion and manipulation.

The good: integrity

Integrity is the extent to which your actions and your statements are aligned. It is linked to honesty and your sense of morality, so integrity is influential. It wins you respect, trust and liking. If I am confident of your integrity, then, at the very least, I will assess your arguments on their merits. I may even decide to accept them as true because I trust you. I am not accepting your judgement; I am accepting *you*.

The bad: coercion

We do what we are forced to do. While everyone will resist coercion, we all have a breaking point. If you have a big enough stick, and you are prepared to use it, then you can gain compliance from anyone. Coercion occurs whenever intimidation or violence is threatened. I believe that compelling acquiescence is appropriate only in the direst emergencies, when people cannot think logically and time is of the essence. It is important to acknowledge that coercion does have a role to play and that some people use it, but that is as far as this book will go in discussing it.

The ugly: manipulation

When your intention is to compel, but you hide it by giving the appearance of free choice, this is manipulation. Here are some examples:

- Using guilt or emotional blackmail:

  "If you don't help out with this, Chris and Sam are going to have to stay late."

- Appealing to their ego:

  "I've always thought you're the smartest one here; we'd have a better chance if you did it."

- Creating fear:

  "If you don't offer me that extra discount, I'll go online and say how bad your company is."

- Playing on our desire to be included, to be liked, or to be loved:

  "You surely wouldn't want to let us all down. We wouldn't appreciate that."

Your choice

If you choose not to demonstrate integrity in your dealings with people, they will come to distrust you and feel your influencing techniques are nothing more than manipulation.

What makes this difficult is finding the boundaries. Where does sincere praise become manipulative flattery? Who is to say that if you let me down badly, I should not resent it? Curiosity is one of our most powerful drivers, so why are adverts that exploit this said to be manipulative, yet the teacher who says "If you want to know, look it up" is just described as trying to create learning skills?

Ultimately, there is only one answer: it is your choice.

 brilliant recap

- Appealing behaviours, like courtesy, generosity and following through on your commitments, speak louder than words.
- Your attitude will influence the people around you, so choose it with care.
- Your determination to cope with setbacks and stay cheerful will help you get the results you want.
- Good preparation will allow you to put a powerful case.
- Integrity is your greatest asset as an influencer.

CHAPTER 2

Appearance matters: how to look influential

> You only get one chance to make a first impression.
>
> My dad (and loads of other people's mums and dads)

Like it or not, we all influence each other by just being who we are. First impressions are a powerful start to this process, so we will start this chapter with why this is true and how to manage your first impression. You will also learn about three other powerful principles:

- the "I'm-gorgeous-fly-me" principle
- the "your-doctor-would-tell-you-to" principle
- the "let-me-introduce-you-to-my-friend" principle.

We will close the chapter by looking at how all this comes together to give some people "presence".

First impressions

The "one-chance-to-make-a-first-impression" principle is unfortunate for the unprepared. However, if you know how important it is, you can harness it to give you instant influence over the people you meet.

Why first impressions matter

Two biases are well known among psychologists who study the way we make decisions. The first is known as the primacy bias. The first information we receive has more impact on our assessment than the things we learn later. I will interpret your behaviour and the things you say in the context of the first thing I find out about you. This is an example of "framing", which means that our first impressions set the context for how we interpret people, information and ideas.

If the first thing I learn about you is an introduction from a colleague, who tells me you are an expert, then that's how I will perceive you. If I don't get that introduction, then as soon as I meet you, I will size you up and make an instinctive judgement. Are you neat or scruffy? Do you look important or insignificant? Do you seem in control or uncertain?

The second bias leads us to notice things that confirm what we already believe to be true. It locks my first impression of you into place, by spotting evidence that supports it – even if my impression is wrong. At the same time, my brain will screen out evidence that contradicts my beliefs, until the weight of that evidence screams at me.

So if you came across to me as uncertain, for example, I will notice every hesitation in your voice and every qualification of your opinion. I will be less inclined to spot when you tell me something important and credit you with the authority you deserve.

How we judge each other

There are six signs that we give each other on first meeting and all of them are under your control: posture, expression, dress, co-ordination, grooming and body language.

Posture

Your posture will tell me a lot about your confidence and your general mood. Good posture sends signals that you are someone who feels in control and comfortable in your environment.

brilliant dos and don'ts for great posture

Do

- ✔ Keep your feet on the floor, pointing at the person you are speaking with. Letting your foot point towards the door or someone else signals an unconscious desire to leave the conversation.
- ✔ Walk with steady, moderately long strides. Hold yourself upright, facing forward.
- ✔ Stand or sit upright, facing directly towards the person you are speaking with.
- ✔ When someone attracts your attention, turn your whole body towards them, rather than just your head or, worse, just your eyes.

Don't

- ✘ Cross your arms: it isn't always a defensive gesture, but is often interpreted as one.
- ✘ Rush: it is a sign of lack of control.
- ✘ Move too slowly: it signals hesitancy and lack of confidence.

Expression

Your expression will back up the message I get from your posture. Consciously, I will notice your expression more, but it is easier to fake and so less persuasive than your posture. However, it is still very important.

The two keys are smiling – it is a sign of confidence and welcomes the other person – and making good eye contact. Good eye contact requires that you hold the other person's eyes for as long as they are comfortable – and no longer. To help you remember to make eye contact, when you shake hands with someone, note the colour of their eyes. This will force you to make eye contact.

When we try to block our expressions, people mistrust us. Beware of covering your mouth or nose with your hands – it sends signals of uncertainty or even lying.

Dress

Dress is first and foremost a social signal. It tells us about status, style and social grouping. The rules today will be out of date tomorrow, and the popularity of clothing shows on television underscores the interest we take in this topic.

Choose your style of dress to conform to the norms of the people you want to influence. This signals that you are like them, so can be trusted. But also move a half notch above them in smartness and quality, to signal your confidence and authority. But be careful: too big a gap can be perceived as arrogance. Equally, don't underdress for an occasion. It is rude and indicates a lack of respect for the people or the context.

If you work in an organisation, look at the successful people around you and emulate their interpretation of the dress code which prevails. Looking different from your peers can equally be seen as a statement of confidence or a statement of rebellion. If people have to get to know you to judge you as influential, then you are missing the opportunity to take a short cut.

brilliant tip

If you are not confident in choosing great clothes, and are not willing or able to hire a style consultant, then look for a trusted friend or colleague who does have a good sense of style and an understanding of what looks right on different people. Get them to offer honest feedback on your choices of style and colour and, if they are willing, ask them to go clothes shopping with you.

Co-ordination

Accessories are the details which are every bit as important as the clothes you wear – and possibly more so. They can make or break your personal impact. So spend money on smart belts, classy jewellery, a stylish notebook, and great scarves or ties. Keep your jewellery and your shoes polished and retire notebooks and briefcases that are looking dog-eared and worn.

In 2004, Parker Pens in the UK released a series of print and outdoor poster adverts. Some showed smart pens, with the slogan "Are you disposable?" Others showed a chewed disposable ballpoint pen, with the slogan "You are what you eat". At the time, the Parker brand strap line was "Aim high".

Watch that your accessories – whether cufflinks or a tie in men, or earrings or a necklace in women – don't attract more attention than you do. If you do wear a joke tie or a bright pair of earrings, be aware that this will send out a message which you may not have intended.

Grooming

Grooming is one of those important details. Get it right and few people will ever notice it. Get it wrong and you will make entirely the wrong impression to everybody.

 brilliant dos and don'ts for grooming

Do

- ✔ Brush and floss your teeth regularly and perhaps even use mints after snacks and meals.
- ✔ Go for a neutral or subtly cologned or perfumed smell. Overpowering people with natural or applied scents is equally unpleasant.
- ✔ Keep your nails clean and trimmed.

✔ Hide unsightly cuts to your hands with discreet plasters.

✔ Look after your hair, keeping it clean and styled.

Don't

✘ Bite your nails in public or leave ragged edges after chewing them in private.

✘ Ignore unwanted hair on your face, neck and ears.

The body language of control

People who feel in control exhibit particular patterns of body language. You can practise these patterns. Here is a list of brilliant do's and don'ts.

brilliant dos and don'ts for control

Do

✔ Sit or stand symmetrically.

✔ Hold your hands palm down, showing the backs of your hands.

✔ Face the other person square on.

✔ Hold eye contact.

✔ Speak steadily and allow yourself to pause.

Don't

✘ Fidget.

✘ Lose your calm.

✘ Slouch.

✘ Point.

✘ Rush.

The source effect

Whenever we get any information, the first thing we do is consider the source of that information. If I tell you I am an expert on influence and persuasion, you may or may not believe me. But if someone else tells you, then when you meet me, you are likely to believe I am that expert. If someone you trust has told you, then you will need very little other evidence. One way to boost your level of influence is therefore to get somebody else – somebody influential – to speak for you.

So if you are asking for somebody's support, or recommending a course of action, then you are the source. How will people evaluate you as a source? They will consider two things: how much they like you, and the extent to which you are a credible authority.

The "I'm-gorgeous-fly-me" principle

Dr Myron L. Fox gave a charismatic lecture, interspersed with humorous asides, to 55 highly qualified psychiatrists, psychologists and social workers. They loved his presentation and rated it as highly thought-provoking. Dr Fox was a fraud. Specifically, he was an actor who had been coached by experimenters to deliver a lecture full of jargon and meaningless content. But he was charismatic, looked distinguished, and he did deliver his lecture very well.

This section covers four topics: what attracts us, how to be likeable, the power of rapport and sensitivity.

What attracts us?

Being likeable is a vital source of influence. It is no coincidence that advertisers choose popular celebrities to promote their product. If I like you, then you will influence me more easily than if I don't know you or don't like you. And if the advertiser cannot afford a celebrity, then they will usually go for someone attractive. Attractiveness creates instant liking. The sad fact is that in experiments with simulated trials, good looking defendants were more likely to be acquitted by a jury, and the less good looking defendants were more likely to be found guilty. So a brilliant tip if you find yourself in front of a jury is to pay attention to your dress and grooming!

How to be likeable

If you have optimised your physical appearance, there are five further things that can make you more likeable: familiarity, compliments, remembering and using names, being sociable, and similarity.

Familiarity

As long as you do not do anything to upset me, one of the easiest ways to make yourself likeable is to make yourself a regular part of my social or working landscape. Far from breeding contempt, familiarity actually begets feelings of comfort and security. We come to like most of the people we work with or socialise with on a regular basis and would far rather take their advice, or buy from them, than from a stranger. People who do a lot of networking as an important part of how they gain business find that typically six to eight meetings with someone will build up the trust that each party needs to recommend the other to their own contacts.

This is also why advertisers create long-running campaigns to build up "brand recognition". When brands or their representatives are familiar, they just feel right to us. Another example is the way that highly polarising politicians of a previous era are, towards the ends of their careers, regarded as elder statesmen and women, who no longer create the strength of negative response in their former detractors. Rarely do their views moderate with age: we are simply more familiar with them. Think of Tony Benn on the left of UK politics and Michael Portillo to the right.

Compliments

When you pay me a sincere compliment, you make me feel good. I will then associate that good feeling with you, and therefore I will like you for it. On the other hand, if I sense that your compliment is insincere, then I will feel that you are trying to manipulate me. You can help your compliments to come across as sincere by making them specific. Rather than say "That was a good report", say instead, "What really impressed me about your report was the logical structure that made it so easy to follow".

But remember, people won't always like you if you always tell the truth. There is no need to lie, but sometimes it pays to hold back a candid opinion.

Using their name

Perhaps the biggest compliment you can pay someone is to remember them. Many people will say that they have "a great memory for faces – but I'm terrible with names". In fact, that is simply how our minds are wired. Remembering names takes more effort; which is why we prize it so highly. However, the effort it takes will be richly repaid. So, whenever you meet someone, make remembering their name a priority.

> whenever you meet someone, make remembering their name a priority

exercise 1   Seven steps to remember a name

1   Pay attention! You have to care enough to make sure you hear and then register the name. As you hear it, repeat it mentally. This will make registering the name a conscious act. Thinks: *"Mike Clayton – OK, got it."*

2   Repeat the name out loud, so it goes through another part of your brain – the speech centres. *"Mike Clayton, hello. I'm pleased to meet you, Mike."* This also gives you a second chance to hear it.

▶

3   Think about it. By processing it mentally, you strengthen the memories. For example, you might spell it out *"M-i-k-e C-l-a-y-t-o-n"* or spot a connection: *"I have a friend called Mark Layton."*

4   Comment on the name to the person you are speaking to. People like you to get their names right, so asking about the spelling is a great approach: *"Is that G-r-a-e-m-e or G-r-a-h-a-m?"* Getting the form of someone's name right is also important: *"Do you prefer Mike or Michael?"* Finally, you can comment on other, appropriate, connections: *"Are you the guy George Clooney played in the movie Michael Clayton?"*

5   Use their name during your first meeting: *"When can we meet properly, Mike?"* People love to hear their name; just don't overdo it like over-familiar shop staff.

6   Make a connection: *"I can see Mike speaking to my Association – that will go down well"*; or visualise pictures in your mind: *"I can picture a ton of clay on a potter's wheel being shaped into a microphone."*

7   Use it one more time as you go your separate ways. "It was great to meet you Mike – do you have a business card?" Well, there's no harm in getting a written record if you can!

Sociability

A willingness to make small talk, to be humorous and to join in with what other people are doing will all make you a popular person to have around, which will also increase your exposure and therefore familiarity. In social clubs and at work, volunteer for discretionary activities and committees. This will give you the chance to get to know other people and be seen to help out.

Similarity

People like people who are like themselves. So look for things you have in common, whether it is a favoured sports team, a city where you have both lived or a hobby you share. One of the commonest similarities people look for in organisations is a common enemy or adversary, whether it is the nasty finance director, the aggressive competitor, or the frustrating photocopier. Clothes are a great way to emphasise similarity too.

People also like people who are like they want to be. We tend to see ourselves not only as we are, but as we want to be, so if you can come across in a way that matches my own aspirations, I will respect you all the more and like you for it.

The power of rapport

To influence someone effectively, you need to start a dialogue. A genuinely two-way exchange relies on rapport; being in sympathy with one another. When you see two people communicating well, you will notice how one person will lean in and the other will do the same. One may pick up a cup of coffee, and so will the other. Rapport is natural, and it looks like a dance. Here are three ways to enhance the natural rapport you have with someone: sincere interest, "someone just like you", and matching and mirroring.

Sincere interest

Showing a sincere interest in what someone is saying will build rapport more quickly than anything else. Asking questions about what is important or interesting to them, and then listening to the answers, will mean that they will instinctively brand you as an excellent conversationalist. Why? Because they will feel you have talked with them about a very interesting subject. If in doubt, the subject that interests people the most is themselves. Asking me about myself will always work!

The more you can learn about me, what is important to me, what I want, and what I need; the better you will be able to frame your propositions to appeal to my self-interest. You will read about this in Chapter 6.

"Someone just like you"

The next way to build rapport is by telling stories. You may want to influence me to believe you understand my situation, you have the products or services I really need, or your suggestion is the best way forward for us. If you were able to tell me a story about someone you know, who is just like me, then I could believe you understand my situation, or have the right products or services for me. If you can tell a story about another, similar situation, I could understand why your suggestion, or your products and services, may be ideal.

Matching and mirroring

Matching is the process of deliberately echoing some aspect of the other person's behaviour. In the section above on similarity, we saw how you can match clothing and look for biographical details in common – even a common enemy. You can go further, by matching aspects of the other person's physiology and speech.

Matching body language

The simplest thing to match is basic posture. If they sit, then you also sit; if they have their legs crossed, cross yours. You could then go on to match subtler aspects of their body language, like some of the gestures they make, the way they hold their head, or the rhythm of movements that they make.

The deepest rapport comes when you match their breathing. There are three things you can match: depth (from shallow, chesty breathing, to deep, abdominal breathing), rate and timing.

Matching speech patterns

As you listen to people, you will notice that some speak more quickly than others. Some people have a distinct rhythm to their speech, whilst others use clipped sentences. Some people speak loudly and some quietly. If I speak slowly and deliberately and you choose a fast-paced style I may crudely characterise you as "fast talking and pushy" which I am sure you are not. On the other hand, if I naturally speak quickly, and you speak very slowly, maybe in my mind, you "don't think as quickly as I do".

So matching the pace, rhythm, volume and even the tone of my voice will help me feel comfortable with you. If, like me, you speak quietly, you are probably also "a sensitive person". If I speak loudly, and you do too, I may feel confident that you too are "bold and confident, like me".

Matching language choices
The final thing you can match is the language I use. At its simplest, you speak the same language as me. But within a language there are lots of different ways we can use the words and grammar available to us. If you spot my preferred styles, then you can use some of them to build rapport. Do I use complex sentences and jargon words, or simple sentences and direct words?

Some people suggest that our use of language also gives away how we like to take in and process information about the world. So, for example:

- Chris may <u>see</u> exactly what you mean. When you explain things <u>clearly</u>, he gets the <u>picture</u>, but if your explanation is a little <u>foggy</u>, then Chris will need to <u>examine</u> your ideas more closely to get them into <u>focus</u> or take a <u>dim</u> <u>view</u> of them.

- When Alex likes the <u>sound</u> of what you are saying it will <u>ring</u> true. If you fail to <u>accent</u> the key <u>notes</u> that she is hoping to <u>hear</u>; then your argument won't have the <u>resonance</u> she needs.

- Sam wants to get a <u>grasp</u> of what you are <u>putting down</u>. If it doesn't <u>feel</u> right, he will know you are only <u>scratching</u> at the <u>surface</u> and your ideas don't have a <u>firm foundation</u>. Even if Sam can't quite put a <u>finger</u> on the problem, he will <u>feel</u> a <u>pressure</u> to <u>push</u> your ideas away.

● Stef <u>understands</u> the <u>context</u> of your argument. When you <u>derive</u> your <u>conclusions</u> from a <u>logical</u> <u>analysis</u> of the <u>data</u> to develop a <u>rigorous</u> <u>conceptual</u> structure, she will <u>appreciate</u> your <u>intellect</u>.

The underlined words are called predicates – they indicate a sensory mode or, in the case of Stef, the lack of one. If Chris really feels more comfortable thinking in images, then using *visual* language will help. In the same way, Alex prefers *auditory* language, and Sam likes *physical* language. If Stef likes an *abstract* way of thinking and speaking, then, if you share that style, she'll find you easier to get on with.

In reality, we all use all of these modes. But listen out for how people use them and if you detect a heavy leaning, or a loud accent towards one or another, then remember to drop a few appropriate words into your talk.

Be careful
Whatever you do – do not overdo this. If it becomes anywhere near obvious to the other person that you are matching them, they will feel that your mimicry is insulting. Having given you this warning, it is surprising how much matching you can do without people consciously noticing it. The best place to practise is in transient public places, like on trains or in waiting rooms.

Mirroring
You may have heard the word "matching" paired with the word "mirroring". In the context of matching or mirroring body language, there is a subtle yet important difference (see Figure 2.1).

Imagine I am sitting with my left elbow and wrist resting across the table and leaning my head on my right hand, with my right elbow on the table. If you sit opposite me and do the same – with your head resting on *your* right hand, then you are matching me.

If you are copying me, but with your head resting on your *left* hand, while your right elbow and wrist are lying across the table, then this is mirroring. What I will see looks, in posture terms, like what I would see in a mirror. This creates more than a simple sense of rapport: it creates a sense of intimacy. Whilst good friends, close colleagues, and even shoppers and sales assistants who are getting on well will match each other naturally, we only start to mirror one another unconsciously when we are forming a deeper bond. So mirroring deliberately will make the other person uncomfortable, if that is not the relationship they want.

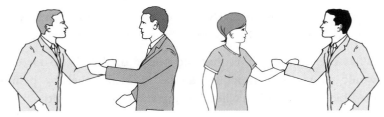

Figure 2.1 Matching (left) and mirroring (right)

Sensitivity is likeable

The last skill to cultivate in being likeable is to be sensitive to the people around you. Start to notice body language: people's posture, gestures and expressions. You don't have to be an expert. You don't even have to read loads of books. Your unconscious mind will start to pick up subtle signals and, when you care, your conscious mind will start to register those signals.

If you notice the other person is uncomfortable, then there is only one thing to do. Change your approach. If you are not yet good enough at interpreting what is making them uncomfortable, then you may get it wrong when you change what you are doing. Don't worry. If you notice they don't seem to be any more comfortable, try something else. The essence of being liked is to take your cue from other people.

The "your-doctor-would-tell-you-to" principle

You would do what your doctor tells you to do, wouldn't you? This is because most people trust their doctor. Three years of pre-clinical training, three years of clinical training and several years of training in their clinical specialty gives doctors the authority to advise you.

In fact, several high-profile news stories show that people will act on a doctor's advice, even if they aren't really a doctor, but are just an amateur, wearing a white coat and masquerading as one. Psychologists have tested this out with controlled experiments and have found that nurses will comply with the instructions of people introducing themselves as doctors, without checking – even when the nurse knows the instructions are dangerous.

What this shows you is that the power of the "your-doctor-would-tell-you-to" principle can be wielded either by being credible or by simply having the appearance of credibility.

Real credibility

True authority comes from genuine expertise and experience. There is no short cut to knowing your business well and gaining the skills and experience of the true expert. However, once you've been through this process, you are fully entitled to show it off. Do this by finding ways to demonstrate your expertise, competence and experience.

Be specific

Experts have depth of knowledge and experience that allows them to call upon detailed evidence to back up their assertions. They also have enough experience to offer real examples to illustrate what they are saying.

Use your experience to tell stories of real and relevant examples that illustrate your point. At all levels of workplace training, people love to hear these "war stories" from experienced trainers. They do the following:

- Communicate directly with the audience – told well, a good and relevant story can hold an audience in rapt silence.
- Make the theory come alive – stories help people to see how the abstract ideas apply to their situation.
- Demonstrate the credibility and authority of the trainer – the example shows that the trainer has real experience.

Offer your qualifications

Some cultures are more concerned with status than others. Germans, for example, value academic qualifications more highly than the British. So when I was working in Germany and went to visit a chemical plant, I thought nothing of the title Dr Mike Clayton on my business card. However, my host, on seeing the card, was immediately concerned that a social blunder was about to ensue: none of the people I was there to meet were PhDs; and I was Herr Doktor. In their culture, this was an insult to me, so frantic calls were made to ensure that the meeting would include one other Doktor. We could then proceed.

Perhaps more common in Western cultures is the importance of rank or job title, so if you have a level of seniority, then letting other people know gives you some instant authority.

Training and professional qualifications are the commonest symbols of authority. If you are a plumber, for example, membership of the Chartered Institute of Plumbing and Heating Engineering (CIPHE) will give you recognition, and registration by the Gas Safety Trust will demonstrate mastery to a specific level of proficiency.

Every trade and profession offers letters to put after your name if you are a member, and most offer a range of membership levels to denote increasing experience and expertise. These usually range from Associate (you are interested) through Member (you have achieved a basic standard) to Fellow (you have eminence in your field).

Educational qualifications are more problematic, because there are so many and their relative "values" are poorly understood at best and poorly defined in many cases. Relevance is the key. If you want to argue for solar power over wind power, your BA degree in medieval history may be of little use. But if I am arguing against you, then my HND certificate in electrical engineering will be more relevant, even though it is a lower level of qualification.

When you are preparing your career résumé, use words like "qualified", "trained", "author of", to highlight your credibility.

The power of testimonials

A testimonial is someone else telling the world how good you are at something. There really is no better way to boost your credibility. Do you remember the source effect, which you saw at the start of this chapter? The more authority the person who gives your testimonial has, the greater the power of the testimonial. If you are a window cleaner and an office manager writes you a testimonial complimenting your work, it will be powerful. If you get a testimonial from the director of facilities, then it will be even better.

Knowing your value

Taste wine from two bottles: one marked at £90 and the other at £10. Which will taste better? When experimenters tried this, volunteers overwhelmingly rated the £90 wine more highly. If you don't think that is surprising, then consider this: both bottles contained the same wine.

Our assessment of the value of something is linked to how its promoters value it. If you set your value at a high level, others will too.

The appearance of credibility

Here is a shocking fact: in many countries, studies show that taller men earn more on average than shorter men. The same is not true for women. Men's height does seem to confer a perception of status among both men and women. Sadly, we cannot alter our height.

It is also true that a deeper voice has the same effect – again something most of us can do little about. Famously, former British Prime Minister Margaret Thatcher had voice coaching to help her lower the tone of her voice. By speaking more slowly, you can control your tone more effectively and also avoid running out of breath (which can send your voice upwards in tone), and so keep your voice at the lower end of its register.

If you are genuinely credible and have the authority you want, there are three principal ways to emphasise it: to look the part, to act the part and to keep quiet.

1. The way you look

Clothing is a powerful indicator of authority. We only have to look back to the "power dressers" of the 1980s with their bold colours and padded shoulders. This should not be surprising. Many male animals emphasise their fitness to defeat rivals and mate with the females with elaborate displays. These range from a deer's antlers to a peacock's tail.

Pinstripes, which accentuate apparent height, go in and out of popularity. But it seems no coincidence that the one place where they are most popular, in the financial districts of major capital cities, are the places with the strongest correlations between male heights and financial remuneration.

If you look the part, people will believe in you. You might be a doctor with a white coat and a stethoscope around your neck, or a business person in a sharp suit. Or you may be carpenter with the right tools at your belt, or a hairdresser with a perfect hair style. Each trade and profession has a certain look and you need a huge amount of credibility to subvert it without diminishing your authority. Only a Bill Gates or a Richard Branson can confidently dare to look like they are off to a family meal when convincing shareholders about investing billions of dollars.

2. Act the part

When you are confident, you inspire confidence in others. Certain patterns of behaviour will control and demonstrate your confidence.

exercise 2

Dorothy Sarnoff was an opera singer, then stage actress, then voice coach, then image consultant. She originated "the Sarnoff Squeeze". This blocks your body's natural production of adrenalin – a hormone partly responsible for the fight or flight response that gives you the sensation of nerves in the pit of your stomach.

1 Sit upright with your back straight, but not rigid, then lean forward slightly.

2 Put your hands together in front of your chest, with your palms together and your fingertips pointing upwards and push.

3 Say "ssssss" as if you were a snake or a leak in a car tyre.

4 As you exhale while saying "ssssss", concentrate on the abdominal muscles below your chest bone, where your ribs begin to spread apart.

5 You should feel these muscles tightening as you exhale.

6 Relax the muscles and inhale slowly.

Once you get good at the Sarnoff Squeeze, you will be able to tighten your abdominal muscles without having to sit in a chair, or push your hands against each other, or even hiss.

If you do this before a stressful event, like an important meeting or an interview, it will help you to feel calmer.

There are three ways to control your confidence: through your posture, visualisation and self-talk (see Figure 2.2).

Figure 2.2 Three ways to control your confidence

Your posture

When you are upright, walking fluidly, with shoulders back and breathing deeply, you will not only look more confident, you will feel more confident. So relax, look straight ahead and allow yourself a little spring in your step.

To show real confidence in a social situation, where you don't know anyone or don't feel able to break into a conversation, rather than stand alone in a corner, find a prominent position where everyone can see you. You are no more alone, but now people will be drawn to you. Only the most confident and charismatic people have the nerve to stand alone in such a visible place.

Double your impact by staying there. Let others come to you and bring you drinks. Now it looks like you have a retinue of admirers: you must be important and influential.

Visualising success

Before entering into a stressful situation, like giving a talk or trying to convince someone important, run through the event in your head a few times. As you run through it, visualise yourself looking and feeling great. See the other person or people visibly impressed by you and persuaded by your argument. See yourself handling objections calmly and effectively. Most important, see the end of the event as a success, with people smiling and congratulating you, and with you feeling like you have achieved what you set out to accomplish.

What this will do is programme your mind to associate the real event with success. You will feel more confident and therefore project more confidence.

Self-talk

The quote "If you spoke to your friends the way you speak to yourself, you'd have no friends" is often attributed to Princess Diana. As you approach a potentially stressful situation, one of the things that can sap your confidence is that nasty little voice in your head. We all have it. When we are feeling bad, it tells us how rubbish we are; when things aren't going well, it tells us it's our fault. But it need not do so. After all, who controls the voice in *your* head? You do.

So, instead of mentally beating yourself up, instil confidence by reminding yourself of all your experience, qualifications and skills. Tell yourself that you are in control and will perform fabulously. Be your own motivational coach.

3. The power of silence

In a Japanese business meeting, the most influential person often says nothing. They sit and listen. When I started working in a consultancy, I saw my boss carrying a huge pilot-style briefcase stuffed with important papers. I thought that signified his importance; and probably so did he. Later in my career, I saw even more senior people carrying a tiny briefcase or even just a portfolio, while I struggled with a laptop, folders and all sorts of stuff. In the world of influence, less is more.

> in the world of influence, less is more

When someone asks you a question or puts their point of view, you will feel a strong impulse to respond as soon as they finish speaking. This may be because you want to show the sharpness of your mind or the degree of your preparation. It may just be because you are, like many people, uncomfortable with silence. Next time, try something different. When the other person stops speaking, allow yourself a few seconds to think.

In that silence, magic can happen. Here are some different ways things can happen:

- The other person may be uncomfortable with the silence, so will fill it with more information. If they are asking a question, they may infer that they were not clear enough. How can you, the master influencer, answer an incomplete question? If they were arguing against you, they may fill the silence by repeating their point. Repetition shows weakness – it sounds like they feel the need to convince you, convince others or just convince themselves. They clearly lack confidence.

- The other person may be comfortable with the silence. So they wait. This builds up expectation for your response. It must be good. You have planted that expectation, so now the confirming bias that you saw towards the start of this chapter cuts in. They hear what they expect to hear.

- Even if the other person is not expecting magic from you, your pause signals that what they said needs careful thought. How much more flattering could you be? A quick answer, on the other hand, sounds like a put down, implying their point was obvious and insignificant. Hardly the way to get them to like you.

- Finally, influential people don't feel the need to rush. At the very least, your pause signifies a confidence in yourself.

A quick comment on the dangers of authority

It is as well to know that people will do almost anything if somebody with sufficient authority asks them to. They feel that if I have the authority to ask, my authority relieves them of the responsibility. Stanley Milgram carried out a number of now famous experiments in the 1960s that demonstrated our tendency to comply, unquestioningly, with the demands of an authority figure. We appear to have a deep-seated sense of duty which has led, throughout history, to abuses of power of unfathomable depths.

The lesson is this: we all have authority over the choices we make. When selecting what actions to take, never relinquish your own authority over the ethics of the choices you make. This is not just a philosophical aside, however. True influence, rather than compulsion, relies on your personal integrity, which must start with acting according to your conscience.

The "let-me-introduce-you-to-my-friend" principle

Let's take a look at another way that you can acquire likeableness and credibility: by borrowing it from other people. This section is about the power of endorsement, sponsorship and patronage. We see these at work everywhere, whether we hear "let me introduce you to my friend" or "my brother is bigger than your brother". We will also look at how your surroundings can lend you an air of authority.

Endorsement, sponsorship and patronage

Advertisers use endorsements from celebrities to associate our liking of the celebrity with their product. They also use experts to endorse their products. All you have to do is watch a few cycles of TV adverts, or flick through two or three magazines and you will have several examples of each.

Sponsorship works in two ways. Commercial sponsors of sporting, charitable or artistic events spend their money to associate their product with our feelings towards the event. If we like a football team, perhaps we will be well disposed to like their sponsor. If we associate an art event with high standards of quality, perhaps that will rub off on to our perceptions of its sponsor. And if a charity event is in aid of a good cause, then its sponsor must be highly ethical and we might then favour them with our custom.

The term "sponsor" refers to someone who takes responsibility for something. In a school or a company, if you have an idea, then you will seek a sponsor at higher levels of your organisation, to back you. In these cases, sponsorship is working in the opposite direction. Now, the sponsor's name and reputation lends credibility to the idea.

This is similar to the way in which patronage works. Charities have prominent people as patrons, so that they can get access to the contacts that the patron can bring. But they may not only use the patron for the value their name brings; if a charity can secure a prominent patron, we may donate to it in the clear knowledge that somebody we like or trust has evaluated the cause for us and lent their name to it.

Sources of power

Power is the ability to get someone to do things regardless of what they want. Each of us has power over the people around us; some have more and some less. In some relationships, that power is balanced: in others, one person's power dominates.

The types of power we can have over others are called "power bases". All these power bases reflect borrowed influence, except for one.

Authentic personal power

This is the one. Your credibility, personality, character and integrity are who you are. The power you get from people's liking, respect and trust is earned, rather than borrowed. Nobody can take it away from you.

Hierarchy power

Organisations and society lend us power when they give us a role and a position. You derive this power from the respect we hold for your position; not from our respect for you. When you lose the position, the power goes with it.

Coercive power

"Speak softly and carry a big stick", said Theodore Roosevelt. If you have a big stick, and you are prepared to use it, you have power.

Reward power

On the other hand, if you are able to reward other people for their contributions, then you can motivate behaviours in a more positive way. This power still relies on access – in this case to the treasure.

Resource power

If you are acting as the gatekeeper to something that I want, then you have power over me, derived from the resources you control.

Knowledge power

Knowledge is a special type of resource. People with specialist knowledge, while it is scarce, wield a lot of power.

Expert power

Knowledge can lose its power as soon as it is published. If I would need experience and skills to apply that knowledge, then your expertise gives you power.

Network power

It is not just what you know, but who you know. With the right network of connections, we can achieve amazing things. That is why networking features in Chapter 9.

Your surroundings

You can also borrow influence from your physical surroundings. Where you choose to hold a meeting can say a lot about you. Watch where politicians are filmed for planned interviews. Locations are typically as follows:

- in front of an imposing and important building – "I have power";
- in a book-lined room – "I am intelligent and knowledgeable";
- in front of a large window – "I have breadth of vision" or even "I am monarch of all I survey";
- in front of a large crowd – "People come to listen to me";
- in schools and hospitals – "I give to the community";
- kissing babies – "I am nice".

If you go to any art gallery, you will see a wider range of surroundings in portrait pictures. Globes, scientific instruments, drapery and even the patterns on fabric all have meanings. When you are trying to influence someone, it pays to consider the image you want to portray and to choose your ground with care.

A modern coffee shop with comfortable chairs says you are relaxed, while a table and upright chairs denotes formality. Sitting facing the door suggests power and putting me with my back to the door will leave me feeling weakened and "exposed". If a group sits on either side of a long table, the meeting can easily become adversarial, while a round table encourages more open debate.

Presence

What is presence? Presence is the indefinable feeling we get from some people when they are in a room. It is a sense that they are there and that we cannot ignore them. They dominate the space they occupy, and people are drawn to them. This magnetism gives them a greater influence: what they say seems to carry more weight and their approval feels important to us.

 **impact**

20 things that will give you presence

Everywhere

1 Confidence.

2 Clothing.

3 Open, symmetric posture.

4 Calm and unrushed.

5 Genuine smiles.

6 Choosing a prominent place and facing the entrance.

With a group

7 Arriving once others are there.

8 Making an entrance.

9 Hands still when you are not speaking.

10 Surveying the space.

11 Avoiding sticking with one person or group.

With an individual

12 Eye contact.

13 Focus – on who you are with.

14 Brief touch to their upper arm (when appropriate).

15 Using silence.

Your message

16 Simple language.

17 Using imagery and metaphor.

18 Speaking clearly and fluently.

19 Looking to the future.

20 Challenging assumptions.

 brilliant recap

- First impressions really matter, so prepare yourself mentally, emotionally and physically.

- Make yourself likeable by offering compliments, smiling, being sociable, remembering names and becoming well known.

- Enhance your likeability by building rapport.

- Demonstrate your credibility with qualifications, testimonials and a confident manner.

- Make use of the people you know and your surroundings to enhance people's attitude to you.

CHAPTER 3

Decisions: how we make them and how we influence them

When you understand how people make decisions, you can influence the decision they will make and how quickly and easily they make their choice.

In the first part of the chapter you will learn how we all look for easy ways to make a decision when the complexity of our choice seems to outweigh the importance of the outcome. We take shortcuts. These shortcuts are wired into the way our brains work, so we are influenced by them even when we really ought to think the decision through with great care. In this sense, we are all the same.

However, we all differ in the criteria we apply to making a conscious decision. The second section of this chapter will look at the different decision strategies we have, and how to spot them, so you can tailor your argument to the people you would like to persuade.

Finally, the chapter closes with a section that will give you processes for getting a decision from somebody.

We are all the same: unconscious shortcuts to decisions

You have already seen two ways that we all make quick assessments to come to decisions. First, there was the "I'm-gorgeous-fly-me" principle. If the person asking us to do something, to buy their goods or to agree with them is someone we like, then we will often just say yes. Knowing we like someone is enough information for us to make small decisions.

Certainly, I shan't buy a house on your recommendation just because I like you, or make a life-threatening decision – although there are probably cases where people have done each of these things. But, if the potential consequences of my decision are small enough, then it is easier for me to say yes than to think it through for myself.

The second reason to say yes without thinking for myself is if your opinion is sufficiently credible for me to trust it without question; this was the "your-doctor-would-tell-you-to" principle. We trust the recommendations of experts. The more expert you are and the more complex the decision, the less I want to make that decision for myself and the more I want *you* to take it for me. Doctors seek "informed consent" when proposing medical treatments. Many people would rather let the doctor decide for them, and a common response is "What would *you* do if you were me, doctor?"

In this section, you will learn about two more of these shortcuts, and how you can use them to influence people: the "eight-out-of-ten-cat-owners" principle and the "sale-must-end-on-Sunday" principle.

The *"eight-out-of-ten-cat-owners"* principle

exercise 3

Go into a busy shopping street with a few friends, spread yourselves amongst the crowd, and wander down the street. If you are at the front, then at some random spot, stop and stare intently at a completely random thing. It may be a piece of chewing gum on the pavement, the bonnet of a parked car, or some guttering at the top of the building. As your friends approach, they should appear to notice what you have noticed and start staring at it too. Soon, other people will stop and stare. They don't know what they are looking at, but it must be interesting and they will try hard to spot it.

It is not just sheep that form flocks; we humans feel a deep need to fit it, to conform. Therefore, when we want to know what to do in a situation, or what to think, we are heavily influenced by the people around us and what they choose to do or think. The more difficult the choice that faces us, the more we will defer to others. This is particularly the case when we need to make a quick judgement, based on very little evidence.

The student and the bystanders

John Darley and Bibb Latane carried out a simple experiment. They had a student accurately simulate an epileptic seizure. Obviously in need of help, if one bystander was around, they would usually help out: 85% of the time, in fact. When five bystanders were there to notice, people offered help at only 31% of the events.

Was the student in real need? When we are on our own, most of us will lend a hand, just in case. When we are together, we look to each other for guidance. During that delay, we may conclude that, since nobody else is helping, they know something we don't.

This effect is known as the "apathy of bystanders", and it can get in the way of you getting the help or support you want. If I think someone else will step in, I will feel comfortable in relinquishing my responsibility to help you.

So, to get my help, you need to break my bond with others who may do nothing. You should let me know that it is *me* that you have turned to, and that I am your best – maybe only – hope.

This will increase the responsibility I feel and overcome my bystander apathy.

Safety in numbers

Another feature of the "eight-out-of-ten-cat-owners" principle is not at all surprising. The more people you can convince, the easier it will be to convince the next one. This is why products and ideas gain momentum and is the basis of one of the most important modern approaches to marketing.

Viral marketing is an approach to popularising a product which relies on potential users spreading the idea "like a virus". It is an extension of word of mouth and works by creating a marketing product that is, itself, so compelling that people will distribute the idea to friends. Some filmed adverts are made never to be shown on television or in cinemas or to be shown once only. The rarity factor (more about this later) and compelling content cause the few people who know about it to seek it out – often on websites like YouTube. They distribute it to friends and the vast numbers of people talking about it add to its prestige.

You can also use this effect powerfully – by using the people you have already convinced to help you convince the people you want to influence. Peer pressure is powerful. Testimonials, which we saw in Chapter 2 as ways to boost your credibility, are also a great way to demonstrate that other people are influenced by you.

People like us

Whose judgement do you trust most? Experts and people you like is the answer you learned in Chapter 2. And if there is a whole crowd of them, then your belief will increase. In the absence of any obvious experts or particular people you like, the next best thing is for the crowd to be made up of people like you.

If the crowd is different from you in some obvious way, then you will subconsciously wonder whether their judgement is relevant.

It is right for them, they are different from you: it is not right for you. On the other hand, if they are the same as you and something is right for them, then it *must* be right for you. Remember, this is an unconscious judgement that you make.

This should remind you, when you present me with testimonials or give me a list of people who are convinced by you, to choose people that I will recognise as being like me.

The "sale-must-end-on-Sunday" principle

Like small children, we want what we cannot have. You can see this principle at work in a number of different forms:

- Unique and rare items have disproportionate value in society.
- When you threaten to remove an opportunity to acquire something, people will feel a pressure to act.
- What society forbids becomes instantly desirable to many of us. Examples include alcohol in prohibition America, or public interest in "secrets" or in news covered by court injunctions.
- Towards the end of a run of a theatre show or art exhibition, people rush to attend.
- Limited edition "collectors' pieces" of porcelain, gold medallions or prints are a booming business.

In summary, things become more attractive as they become less available.

Contradiction

This "sale-must-end-on-Sunday" principle seems to conflict with our previous "eight-out-of-ten-cat-owners" principle. In the one, we want what nobody else has and, in the other, we want what everybody has.

We do indeed have two ways of deciding on value: if everybody wants it, it must be valuable; and also, if it is rare, it must be valuable. Perhaps what is going on here is that, knowing something is rare, we infer that everybody *must* therefore want it. Now the two principles work together.

Using rarity to influence others
If you recall Chapter 2, you learned that familiarity is one of the things that can make you seem more likeable. As people encounter you or your products a lot, they start to feel comfortable with them. Once you are liked, however, this new principle shows you that remaining too available will diminish your influence. People will crave your presence more if you are less available.

> integrity means fulfilling every commitment that you make

Integrity means fulfilling every commitment that you make. Once you have built liking, it is time to reduce the number of commitments you make. When you say no strategically, it makes your support or assistance harder to come by and therefore more highly valued.

People who say yes too often, even when it does not suit them, will no longer be more and more liked, but will become less and less respected: they risk becoming a "doormat". When you say no for a good reason, I will continue to like and respect you for your honesty and integrity. You are not a pushover; you are someone who thinks carefully before offering a commitment.

Using rarity to get things done
Many people need deadlines to really get them going. By making time a precious commodity, you can trigger my need to seize that commodity and use it well. Be careful how you use deadlines; they also work on fear, one of the most powerful of our emotions. Using fear of failure to gain compliance can be manipulative, so make sure you also secure agreement to the deadline, rather than impose it on somebody.

As an example, project managers negotiate multiple deadlines to create momentum among team members. Time is always scarce, so there is always a pressure to hit your target. They call their deadlines "milestones" – a much more pleasant metaphor.

We are all different: how different people make decisions

If we were truly all the same, then the art of influence would be easy and we would all be good at it. The variety of ways with which we each respond to influence make it a more complex skill. In this section, you will learn more about the different ways that people make decisions. We will first see what it takes to convince people and then we will examine five personality types and how each one makes decisions.

What does it take to convince you?

When I consider an important decision carefully, a whole raft of factors will influence my choices. Your task, in influencing my decision, is to give me information on all those factors and to focus on the ones that are most important to me. The mistake most of us make when influencing is, rather than focusing on what will persuade the other person, we present the information that *we* find most compelling.

How you represent your information

You read in Chapter 2 how we each make language choices: visual, auditory, physical or abstract. These are echoed in the way we like to evaluate options. We all use each of the four approaches, but some people have a clear preference for one or two.

- Chris likes visual language, so convince him by showing pictures and diagrams. Let him see the clarity of your argument for himself.

- Alex likes auditory language, so convince her by letting her discuss your ideas and hear the tone of your arguments for herself.

- Sam likes physical language, so convince him by letting him try things out and test the strength of your arguments for himself.

- Stef likes abstract language, so convince her by letting her read the facts and figures so she can understand the logic of your arguments herself.

How hard you have to try

Have you ever noticed that some people make an instant decision? When you have given them the information they need, they have instantly decided "That's it, I've got it, what next?" Anything you add now will, at best, frustrate them and, at worst, lead them to doubt their decision.

Other people need a drip feed of information over a period, before it settles into their consciousness and they feel ready to take a decision. Trying to get a quick decision from them will probably undermine your personal influence and could very well cause them to reject your argument outright.

Finally, some people don't so much need lots of information, they just need time. Their decision process is no less instinctive than the first group; it just takes them longer to feel comfortable with the decision they need to make. The bigger their decision is, the longer they need. Rushing them will only serve to slow them down, by making them feel less comfortable.

What criteria to present

Think back to a time when you made an important buying choice. What finally made you decide on what you bought, and reject other options? There are four factors that come up repeatedly:

- *Cost.* For some people this is always critical; yet, for others, it is only a marginal consideration unless affordability is in question.

- *Quality.* Some people must have things absolutely right and are prepared to pay a premium for "perfect". Others are happy with "good enough" – as long as the product meets a minimum requirement.

- *Risk.* For some people, the possibility of making a mistake dominates their choice and they will play it safe. They may also find it hard to make a choice at all.

- *Availability.* As we have seen, some people are drawn to something because it is rare and hard to get. Others are drawn to something they can get easily without much fuss – they are in a hurry.

Five personality types

If we put all this together and throw in our different responses to other aspects of influence, we arrive at the infinitely rich diversity of human decision making. To simplify this, here are five easy-to-recognise decision-making styles:

- "How would you do it?" – following people.
- "It needs to excite me" – ideas people.
- "Prove it to me" – analytical people.
- "I'm listening to my gut" – intuitive people.
- "We'll do it my way" – controlling people.

"How would you do it?" – following people

A lot of people only feel safe if they are doing what others do. The "eight-out-of-ten-cat-owners" principle works fabulously well with them. They are therefore easy to influence, once you have built up other people's support. They are particularly reliant on people who are close to them and whom they trust, so get to know these key influencers and invest time in them. Better still, become one of these following people's trusted advisers yourself. Following people are likely to be cautious and go for a safe option, rather than take a risk, so emphasise track record and reliability.

↗ **brilliant** tactics to persuade following people

● Emphasise proofs.

● List existing supporters.

● Cite examples and track records.

● Compare to trusted ideas, brands, approaches.

● Offer guarantees or show how risk is minimised.

● Use words like reliable, popular, tested, similar, proven, certainty.

● Take your time – following people dislike pressure and distrust change.

One final irony you should be aware of: following people rarely see themselves that way. They would like to be innovators, but lack the courage to take controlled risks. So, if you can show them how your idea is safe and tested in one context, and yet they will be the first to adopt it in their own context, they will love it.

"It needs to excite me" – ideas people

Ideas people are prepared to take a risk, as long as the potential benefit is sufficiently enticing. But they are not gamblers; they will scrutinise your proposal with care. If they do adopt it, they will commit 100%. They will come across as charismatic and enthusiastic and, while they can think quickly, they often reserve the right to consider their options for a while.

↗ brilliant tactics to persuade ideas people

- Focus on results, benefits and controls.
- Start with the big picture but be ready with details.
- Keep it real – being overly conceptual will cause doubts.
- Let them drive the discussion with their questions and ideas.
- Don't labour a point – if they say they've got it, move on.
- Use words like action, focus, results, benefits, convenient, straightforward.
- Visual aids and visual language will often appeal to them.

"Prove it to me" – analytical people

Analytical people are hard work, because their personal preference for logic and facts means that they avoid the shortcut decisions that will help you influence other people. Chapter 5 focuses on their needs. Be prepared for fearsome logic and a requirement for large amounts of rigorous data. They will challenge your thinking and your evidence and can come across as rude and impersonal.

↗ brilliant tactics to persuade analytical people

- An academic style of presentation works well, using research, case studies, statistics and comparative data.
- Make the logic of your argument absolutely rigorous.
- Have all the details to hand.
- Present options and show you have considered them all from multiple angles.
- Address the risks – analytical thinkers like to remove as much risk as they can.

- Use words like expert, evidence, data, quality, research, analysis, facts, rigour, logical.
- Give them time to think, figure it out for themselves, and make their considered decision.

"I'm listening to my gut" – intuitive people

Some people draw upon all their life experiences in making their decisions but, rather than do it in a logical way like analytical people, they access their experience as gut instinct and intuition. If you challenge their thinking, you are challenging them, so work on rapport building and stress your credibility and the similarities in your perspective. Intuitive people tend to be blunt, inward-focused people who are proud to speak their mind. You will need to flatter them to a degree and plant the information they need, so they can feel it is part of their own world view.

↗ brilliant tactics to persuade intuitive people

- Build your credibility with them by showing you can see things from their perspective and have testimonials from people they trust.
- Avoid challenging them head on, and be prepared for a powerful rebuff if your ideas don't fit their experience.
- Root your arguments in experience.
- Use case studies and personal stories.
- Use physical language and create opportunities for them to get some hands-on experience.
- Allow them to save face if you need to correct them.
- Use words like feel, grasp, grip, trust, instinct, honest, integrity, solid.
- Be prepared for a sudden decision that will not change.

"We'll do it my way" – *controlling people*

Controlling people like to think that they cannot be influenced. If they think an idea is yours, then they will mistrust it. If they adopt it anyway, and it goes wrong, steel yourself for blame and retribution: controlling people can be dominant, domineering and downright aggressive. They are mainly hard to influence, because they would rather talk than listen, so let them lead the agenda. Not surprisingly, they need to feel in control, so risk-taking is not a strength: give them clear and detailed plans.

⟍)brilliant tactics to persuade controlling people

- Find ways to help them think of an idea for themselves.
- Don't push your idea, let them pull it from you.
- When you answer questions, be straightforward, logical and direct.
- Focus on facts rather than opinions (they don't value anybody's opinions but their own).
- Avoid ambiguity and confusion.
- Use words like reason, best, logic, action, control, strength.
- Many controlling people need to control to manage their own fears – without referring to fear, show how they can make a safe decision that bolsters their power and authority.

Getting a decision: processes that work

There are three steps to getting a decision:

1 Give the right information.

2 Spot the signals.

3 Ask for the decision.

Give the right information

You have seen in the last section of this chapter that different people need different information to make their decision; and they need it in the right format. So the first step in getting a decision from me is to pay attention to what I want and to match your influencing style to my decision-making style.

It is important not to give too many options if you want a decision. When I have more options to evaluate, I will worry that I have more chances of choosing the wrong one. Limiting my options will help me to make a decision.

Spot the signals

When people are ready to make a decision, their language, behaviour and body will tell you. Watch out for deliberate and unconscious indications.

Deliberate behaviours

If I am interested in what you are saying, I will consciously take an interest. I might:

- ask clarifying questions;
- encourage you, nod and even agree with you;
- ask your advice or what the next steps are;
- take notes;
- focus on details – I might even challenge you on these details;
- ask "What if ... ?"

Unconscious signals

Even if I don't choose to encourage you, I may not be able to control some of these signs:

- leaning towards you;

- matching your posture and vocal tone;

- direct language such as "I like it" signals enthusiasm; indirect language such as "It's a nice idea" signals reserve;

- use of I, we or us indicates commitment;

- elaborating on your ideas;

- a closed hand resting on the cheek, with the index finger pointing upwards suggests they are interested in what you are saying – but if they rest their chin on their thumb, they have doubts;

- stroking the chin suggests that their mind is occupied with decision making – if they then lean forward, the answer is yes; if they lean back, then it is no.

Ask for the decision

The biggest mistake that inexperienced negotiators make is not asking for a decision at the right time. Many a sale has been lost by a nervous salesperson who has rapport and fears that asking for the deal will break the spell. So, instead, the nice meeting ends without a sale and both people feeling a little let down.

> the biggest mistake that inexperienced negotiators make is not asking for a decision at the right time

Here are six ways to ask for a yes.

The direct ask

"Do you agree with … ?" "Can you agree to …?" "Shall we shake hands on it?"

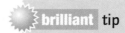 **brilliant** tip

Signing a contract feels like *big deal*. So instead of saying, "Would you sign this contract?" how about saying "Would you just OK this paperwork?"

"Paperwork" sounds a lot less threatening than a "contract" and "OKing" it feels far less official than "signing" it. Finally, did you spot that extra little word: "just"?

The summary and ask

Soften them up by summarising the points of agreement: "So, we have agreed ... and ... Are you now able to support me on this?" Notice the word "now". If they can't support you now, the door is still open for tomorrow.

The conditional ask

If you sense that they are close to agreeing and you want to know how close, try something like this: "If I were to ..., could you then agree to ... ?"

The one more ask

A nice variant on this is to ask what one issue you would need to satisfy or thing you would need to do to get agreement.

The presumptive ask

Here is a way to ask without asking, by presuming you know the answer and asking a different question. The answer to this question will indicate agreement, or not: "So, when would you like to get started?"

The either-or ask

Offering two options, both of which constitute a good result for you, gives the other person a choice, and makes it easy to agree, without having to "give in". "When would you like to tidy your bedroom: before supper or after supper?"

 **recap**

- We are heavily influenced by what other people think. Use the "eight-out-of-ten-cat-owners" principle to boost your influence.

- Things are more desirable when they are hard to get. So ration your availability and use the "sale-must-end-on-Sunday" principle.

- Different things convince different people. Get to know how each person makes their decision and choose your influencing style accordingly.

- A three-step process will help you get a decision:

  1 Give the right information.

  2 Spot the signals.

  3 Ask for the decision.

CHAPTER 4

Understand the psychology of influence

Powerful influence over other people arises from the way their brain works. To master influence, you need a good working knowledge of some critical aspects of our psychology. This chapter addresses seven new topics that are not explored earlier in this book. Each will add to your resources in getting what you want.

Cognitive dissonance – the "Jiminy Cricket" effect

In Walt Disney's *Pinocchio*, when the Blue Fairy realises that Pinocchio cannot stop himself from lying, she appoints Jiminy Cricket as Pinocchio's conscience, to help him to tell right from wrong, avoid great temptations, and guide him along the right path.

Conscience is an inner voice that tells us what is right and what is wrong. When we are about to do something that is inconsistent with our conscience, we feel uneasy about. That feeling of unease is what psychologists call "cognitive dissonance".

Self-image

One of the strongest drivers of our behaviour is how we see ourselves. If your self-image is as a diligent person who gets things done on time, no matter who asks you, then that self-image will do what you promised.

one of the strongest drivers of our behaviour is how we see ourselves

Whilst we accumulate our self-image through a lifetime of experiences and choices, there are ways to influence people's perception of themselves. Recent experiences weigh particularly heavily on our self-image. They may not counter a lifetime of perceptions, but stacking sufficient new experiences can overwrite an out-of-date image. This is the basis of a range of therapies.

We often hear that you need to change attitudes before you can change behaviours. In fact, it will work the other way around and is the basis of one of product marketers' favourite approaches: "try before you buy". What marketing professionals know is that if you can influence someone sufficiently to change a behaviour, the new behaviour can alter somebody's self-image.

Good examples of this approach in action are:

- Encouraging a child to spend just one night camping can lead them to start to think of themselves as adventurous.

- Persuading a junior manager to make their first short presentation to peers will help them think of themselves as a presenter.

You can gauge a measure of the strength of a self-image from the way that people talk about themselves. Compare the colleague who tells you they like to run at the weekend with another who tells you that they are runner who trains at weekends. One has told you about their behaviour; the other has also told you about their sense of identity as a runner.

Making commitments

One of the strongest influencing techniques is to actively engage the potential for cognitive dissonance. Very few people think of themselves as deceitful, inconsistent or dishonourable. You can use this powerful self-image that most of us have of honesty and integrity to improve the likelihood that someone will comply with a request.

Rather than simply asking me to do something, ask me to confirm that I *will* do that thing. Make sure you wait until I give you an answer. Once I have said yes, my Jiminy Cricket circuit has been primed. To not do that thing will set up cognitive dissonance – a feeling of unease because there is conflict between two things:

- my self-image as reliable and honourable;
- my knowledge that I have made a commitment.

I now have two ways to reduce my inner conflict. I can rationalise my lack of action by finding a sufficient excuse that will allow me to remain consistent with my self-image, or I can just get on and do it. In many cases, the latter course will be the easier and I will get on with what I have promised.

Two factors will enhance the power of my commitment:

1   The more public that commitment is then the stronger its effect will be – get them to commit in front of other people.

2   The more permanent that commitment is then the stronger its effect will be – get them to put their commitment in writing or put their name to it.

You can further enhance this effect by setting a specific time-frame, so that Jiminy Cricket knows when to start bugging them. Also let them know the consequences to you or other people if they let you down, so Jiminy can also bug them about the effect of their failure.

One step further is to cite a generic value identity, saying something like: "It's amazing how some people can make a promise and then discard it lightly." This now transforms compliance with a commitment into a test of character. Who would want to fail that!

▶ **brilliant** example

If you want me to think more highly of you or accept your recommendation, or do something for you, first ask me to do you a favour. It does not need to be a big favour, as long as I have to put myself out for you in some way.

This may sound paradoxical – especially if you have read Chapter 7 and know that doing me a favour is likely to influence me to reciprocate.

The technique works because when I do you a favour, I am demonstrating that I value you in some way. To avoid cognitive dissonance, I must continue to act consistently with that decision. So, the giving *and receiving* of favours both increase your influence.

Expectation – the "doing what's expected" effect

People tend to do what is expected of them. So if you act or ask with enough confidence, they will be likely to do what you want. This approach is based on our need to conform, which can often lead us to act without thinking.

For example, if you want to get a group of friends to follow you down the left fork, just head off down the path without looking back; perhaps saying "We'll take this path". If you say and do this with absolute conviction, some will immediately follow you and that will create a herd effect that we saw in Chapter 3. On the other hand, if you turn back, look doubtful, and ask "Are you coming?" you will encourage people to question your lead.

Our expectations extend to things as well as people. If you expect something to be really hot – such as a radiator – you might touch it gingerly to find out if it is on or not. For a fraction of a second, you might fancy you felt the heat, despite it being off and cold.

Medical science is well aware of the "doing what's expected" effect and in medicine it is known as the placebo effect. Drugs and treatments can effect a reduction in symptoms and, in certain cases, a cure, despite there being no active ingredient in the medicine or no therapeutic value to the treatment. Less familiar to non-medically trained people is the opposite effect: the nocebo effect. A negative expectation of a drug or treatment can create an undesired effect in a patient. The term is often extended to any patient deterioration that can best be ascribed to a belief that their condition will worsen. Perhaps the most widely known example is the way voodoo can cause psychosomatic illness.

What all of this shows is the awesome power of our minds. The greater the level of credibility that you can portray, the stronger this effect will be. Medical doctors do have a large bank of authority, arising from their training, status and the badges of their trade. Not surprisingly, the way they speak with and treat their patients alone can influence some therapeutic outcomes.

This is, perhaps, the ultimate form of influence. Great leaders can only be leaders because people are prepared to follow them. This aspect of our personality shows that we all want to be led.

Reactance – the "black is white" effect

 To every action there is always an equal and opposite reaction.

Sir Isaac Newton's third law of motion in
Philosophiæ Naturalis Principia Mathematica
(the Principia)

Rather like inanimate objects, human beings react to an imposed force, and the more pressure put on us, the more we resist. If we feel our freedom of choice or action is being limited, we will oppose that force. This is called reactance.

if we feel our freedom of choice or action is being limited, we will oppose that force

Reactance accounts for a pervasive attitude that frustrates us all. Commonly called the "jobsworth" attitude, it occurs when people with an official role take the view that doing something is "more than my job's worth". The harder you push them to make a concession, the more they resist.

The secret, of course, is not to push because doing so can easily result in the other person doing precisely the opposite of what you want. This is prevalent in us all; not just in toddlers and teenagers.

Helping people to comply

Imagine you arrive at a car park in a desperate hurry for an important meeting. Unfortunately, every space seems to be full. As you consider whether to risk double-parking, you spot the car park attendant watching you carefully, from a spot where there is just enough room for your car – even though it is not a marked space. What should you do?

The first thing to do is to let them know that *they* have the final decision and that you will respect the choice they make. This means that they have nothing to react against; unlike the alternative of demanding their help or telling them what *you* would do. When you have done this, set out the relevant facts, including an acknowledgement of the disadvantages as well as advantages of the action you are requesting: "I know there must be a reason why that space is not a marked parking space." Since they already know the disadvantages, your openness will come across as a concession. Finally, appeal for their help: "I really am in a bit of a fix, so I really would be grateful if there were anything you could do to help me out."

To take this one step further, an additional way to help people comply rather than resist is to ask them to imagine a future in which they have done what you asked. This has the effect of making the possibility seem more real. If, for example, you want a colleague to take some time out of their own work to help you prepare for a presentation, you could ask them how they would feel if, between you, you produce a really first-class piece of work that has a significant impact on your company's future.

Salespeople often use this approach. You are shopping for a new television and the shop assistant starts by showing you the top-of-the-range model. They might ask you: "Just imagine how you'll feel, relaxing on your sofa, enjoying such a great picture quality and such powerful and clear sound. Do you like movies, sport or documentaries?" You cannot help but answer their question in your mind, and "pow" – into your mind pops an image of yourself watching a broadcast on this great new TV. You want it now.

The credibility paradox – the "narrower is deeper" effect

"Hi, I'm Mike and I am an expert in everything."

"Hi, I'm Mike and I am an expert in influencing and persuading."

"Hi, I'm Mike and I am an expert in workplace influencing and persuading."

"Hi, I'm Mike and I am an expert in workplace influencing and persuading, at managerial level."

"Hi, I'm Mike and I am an expert in writing workplace reports that influence and persuade managers."

As you read this list of alternative introductions, which one seems the most persuasive? For most people, it will be the last one. Paradoxically, the narrower you claim your expertise to be, the more credible and influential you become. To be influential, find yourself a niche.

One reason that this works is the "power of the specific". The narrower and more particular a claim is, the less we tend to question it. We assume that, because the claim has been honed to a high level of precision, it must be correspondingly accurate. Of course, precision and accuracy are two very different things, but our brains frequently take a shortcut and miss the distinction.

> the narrower and more particular a claim is, the less we tend to question it

But, you are wondering, does that not limit the breadth of your influence? Not at all. Once we build a respect for somebody, we tend to extend that respect into other areas with little or no evidence. Celebrities often lend their name to advertising campaigns. Just because somebody is renowned as sportsperson, it does not mean that their business judgement or their choice of cosmetics is particularly well informed.

Decision fear – the "too much choice" effect

When you have no option, it is easy to decide what to do. As the number of options before you increases, so does the difficulty you face in making a decision.

When you have to make more of an effort to make a decision, the prospect of getting that decision wrong seems more uncomfortable. Therefore, as the number of options you have increases, not only does the difficulty of making a choice grow; so do the consequences of getting it wrong.

The result of this is that if you offer somebody too many choices, they will be less likely to make a decision; instead, they will put off the decision.

We want choice ...

This conclusion seems contradictory. Years of psychological research shows that people actually want more choice. Indeed, many brands compete by offering their potential customers a wider range of options than their competitors. Two researchers called Sheena Iyengar and Mark Lepper got to the bottom of what is going on here.

Wilkin & Sons make a huge range of jams and conserves and some specialist grocers stock them all. The two researchers found one such store in California and set up tasting booths in the store, which allowed shoppers to taste as many jams as they liked. Some shoppers saw a booth with 24 of the more exotic flavours of jam, and others saw a booth with just six of those flavours.

The booth offering the smaller choice of six jams attracted 40% of the shoppers to try jams, each trying an average of 1.4 jams. The big booth with the wider range of jams attracted 60% of shoppers to taste jams and they each sampled an average of 1.5 jams.

What this seems to show is we *do* prefer more choice – shoppers were more likely to stop and sample from the wider choice.

... or we think we do

Iyengar and Lepper did one more thing at their booths. They gave everybody who tried a jam at either booth a voucher for a $1 discount on any of the Wilkin & Sons range of jams. By coding the vouchers, they could track buying patterns of people who had sampled from the big booth or the small booth. The results were startling.

Out of 104 people who sampled jams from the small choice booth, 31 of them (30%) subsequently bought a jam with their voucher. However, of the 145 shoppers who stopped and tasted jam at the big booth, only four of them (fewer than 3%) actually bought a jam.

In subsequent experiments, the researchers looked at some of the factors that might have confounded this study. Their final conclusion is that too much choice, while appealing, does indeed hinder decision making.

Limit choice

When you want to get action from someone, you must limit their choices. Give them enough choice so that they feel in control, but not so much that they feel that making a decision is too hard and they are too likely to get it wrong.

Imagine you are shopping for your first digital camera. If you go into a shop that offers you six well-chosen models, we know that you are more likely to buy than if the shop stocked a range of 24 different models. We also know that if there were two such shops side by side, you would probably go into the better-stocked shop. So the solution is to stock a wide range, and then create a display offering a more limited choice to those who do not feel expert enough to understand the whole range.

Limit information

Another factor contributes to our discomfort with decision making: too much information. Think back to our camera store: how much information should the store owner give you about each camera?

We make decisions most quickly and most confidently when we have a small amount of salient information. More information confuses us or introduces doubt. When trying to influence behaviour, your task is to give a small amount of relevant information to support decision making.

Comparisons – the "black and white" effect

Artful use of comparisons is an important skill for an influencer. Human beings seem predisposed to consider things in the context of other things around them. For example, people are perfectly happy with what they have, whether it is their car, home, or salary, until they learn that the person next to them has something more or better. You can use this effect to your advantage.

One thing and another

Many people have had an experience of buying an expensive piece of equipment they wanted (like a stereo or a car) and then finding themselves buying a few small extras that they would probably never have needed. It may be software or a mouse for your new computer, a shirt or blouse to go with the new suit you just chose, or even an extra memory card for that new digital camera you bought (from the shop with six cameras on special offer, each of which had two great reasons why it is best for a particular type of use).

When you are spending £100, an extra £8.99 does not seem a lot and salespeople are adept at using this principle. It works in other contexts too:

● "While you are writing that 50-page report, could you do me a two-page summary for the website?"

● "Thank you for granting me three weeks' extended leave for my honeymoon; would it also be OK to have next Friday off so my partner and I can go and speak with our caterers?"

Notice how these also make use of a previous commitment, to make it harder to say no to a second, consistent, request.

One thing and another, and another

The camera shop has three models of digital camera on special offer:

● the Lumo 350, for £84.99;

● the Penton C600 for £128.50;

● the Candid XLP for £169.00.

All three cameras do what you need but they all have slightly different specifications. Which one will you buy? It turns out that more than half of people in your situation would buy the middle-priced model. When restaurants add a new main course to their menu that has a higher price than any other, they may not sell very many of them, but sales of other high-cost choices go up, as does the average value of a meal ordered.

When you are offering me options, it makes sense to use the comparison effect to make your middle option more attractive, by offering me a "top" option that you do not expect me to select.

One thing and another, or both

The "black and white" effect has one last trick up its sleeve. Dan Ariely is a Professor of Behavioural Economics. So he was intrigued by an advert for *The Economist*. It offered three options:

1 online subscription: $59;

2 print subscription: $125;

3 print and online subscription: $125.

He decided to ask his students which they would go for. Of 100 students, 16 opted for the online subscription, none opted for the print subscription and 84 opted for the two subscriptions together.

Since none opted for option 2, he decided to see what would happen if he did not offer that option, so he offered options 1 and 3 to another 100 students. This time, something strange happened. Only 32 of them went for the double subscription and 68 opted for the online subscription only.

This is not rational behaviour (Ariely's book is called *Predictably Irrational*). In the absence of option 2, students are weighing the added benefit of the print copy and fewer than a third of them find it justifies the extra $66. When option 2 is available, most students see option 3 as getting something for nothing and jump at the bargain. That's brilliant!

Pattern interrupts – "shock, awe and laughter"

A moment of confusion, when you can break someone's thought pattern, is an opportunity to influence them.

brilliant example

In an early experiment that demonstrated this, researchers rode crowded New York subway trains. They tried two approaches to getting a seat from people who already had one:

1 Researchers mentioned to a fellow passenger that they were thinking of asking someone to give up a seat for them.

2 Researchers spontaneously asked people: "Excuse me; may I have your seat?"

The success rate for the first approach was 28% and for the second, it was twice that, at 56%.

Confusion

There is an old saying among salespeople: "If you can't dazzle them with brilliance; baffle them with nonsense." It turns out from research since the late 1990s that this is literally true. If, during a sales pitch, you make a confusing or nonsensical statement, then complete the pitch with a reason to buy, you will increase the proportion of people who will buy.

The most quoted example is in the sale of a package that costs $3.00. When researchers told customers that the price was $3.00, 40% of customers bought it. However, when they told customers that the pack was "300 pennies, which is a bargain", sales went up to 80%.

It seems that the momentary confusion of hearing something absurd creates an increase in the amount of work our brains have to do and therefore depletes our ability to analyse the offer. When we hear the "hook" or the reason to buy ("which is a bargain"), this triggers compliance through the power of "because", as you will shortly see, in Chapter 5.

You will need to be cautious when using this approach, however. If you throw in too much incongruity, it will be very noticeable at a conscious level and also distract from the hook.

Shock

If someone is behaving unreasonably, then there is a good chance that reasoning with them will not influence their behaviour. Sometimes you need to drop a bomb on their unconscious mind and interrupt the unreasonable pattern. A favourite trick of one therapist, when he senses a client getting hysterical, is to "accidentally" spill a cup of water all over the table between them. Most people have a reflex-like instinct to try to mop up the mess which, for our therapist, is just what he wants because it interrupts the unhelpful response.

Strange as it may seem, sometimes a well-chosen use of shouting, swearing or physical gesture can change behaviour radically.

Humour

The nicest way to interrupt our thought patterns is with humour. Jokes and other humorous comments or actions all produce a moment of surprise that catch us off guard.

Not only does the humour charm us and trigger likeability; it also signals confidence and hence credibility. It is hard to be genuinely funny when we feel challenged or stressed.

If you use humour, you will gain my attention, distract my mental processes, make yourself likeable and show a confident presence. Humour is a powerful part of the influencer's toolkit.

brilliant recap

- We feel a need to do what we say we will do, or we suffer the consequence of our conscience telling us off. Use this to good effect by asking people to make a formal commitment to you.

- We also do what is expected of us. If you act with enough certainty, people will follow your lead.

- If you apply too much pressure, however, people will react against it and refuse to comply.

- The narrower your expertise, the more people are inclined to believe in it. It pays to be a specialist.

- Too much choice stifles decision making, so give limited amounts of choice to get a quicker and more confident decision.

- Taking people by surprise gives you a chance to influence th͏ behaviour. You can do this using confusion, shock or hum͏

PART 2

Your message

CHAPTER 5

The importance of what you say

You may be tempted to believe that, with the right techniques, you can influence anybody to do or believe anything. Happily, this is not true. Substance matters enormously: the rigour of your ideas, the quality of your products, the value of your proposals, or the implications of your requests.

This chapter is about how to structure your argument to give it the maximum impact. It includes:

- the importance of good evidence;
- how to hook the person or people you want to influence with a compelling opening statement;
- how to order your argument in a persuasive sequence;
- how to complete your message with a powerful close.

Influence through reason

Human beings have a deep need for reason and purpose. This is illustrated by the favourite question of small children: "Why?" Most of us may grow out of asking this question every day (with the exception of scientists), but it is still there in our minds. When you link your request to a reason, you are more likely to get a "yes" response.

▶ brilliant example

Would you do a favour and let someone go ahead of you when you were about to use a photocopier? Helen Langer, Arthur Blank and Benzion Chanowitz did an experiment in 1978. They asked 120 students if they could use a library photocopier first, just after the student had reached it. The experimenter asked in three different ways:

1   "May I use the Xerox machine?"
     Giving no reason.

2   "May I use the Xerox machine, because I have to make copies?"
     Giving no real reason.

3   "May I use the Xerox machine, because I'm in a rush?"
     Giving a reason.

When the request was a small one – the experimenter had only five sheets to copy – 9 out of 15 (60%) of the students asked obliged without hearing a reason (Request number 1). With a reason (Request Number 3), 15 out of 16 (94%) agreed. Here's the surprise – with no real reason (Request number 2), 14 out of 15 (93%) were prepared to oblige. The reason is clearly not important; what was important was that there was a reason – the students heard the word "because" and that was enough.

Is "because" sufficient in all cases? No. When the experimenter made a bigger request, to copy 20 pages, only 6 out of 25 students (24%) obliged with both of questions 1 and 2. With a real reason, however, 10 out of 24 students (42%) were prepared to be generous. So to agree to a significant request, we need a significant reason.

Get your content right

You must be prepared for your evidence to be analysed with forensic precision. Not because it always will be but because it may be. If it is, the smallest error can wholly undermine your credibility.

Mark Antony's principle

 The evil that men do lives after them,
The good is oft' interred with their bones;

Mark Antony in *Julius Caesar*, by William Shakespeare

In a 100-page report, what the finance director is most likely to remember is the error in line 6 of the table on page 37. This error has the power to compromise the FD's confidence in the rest of the document, including your recommendations.

The Pareto principle

Vilfredo Pareto was an Italian economist at the start of the twentieth century. He observed that 80% of the land in Italy was owned by 20% of its population. Globally, the same pattern is very much present today (see Figure 5.1). This has become known as the 80–20 rule but there is nothing special about those numbers.

What is generally true in many situations is that the majority of the impact comes from a small number of key components. When you want to influence somebody, a dozen arguments are of little value. The impact comes from one or two compelling arguments.

impact comes from one or two compelling arguments

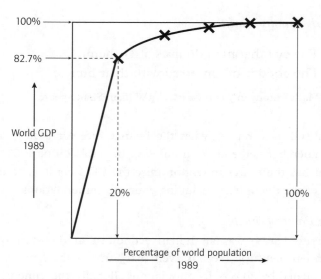

Figure 5.1 The Pareto principle

The journalists' principle

A common expression in journalism is: "Slaughter your dar-
lings." It means: eliminate everything that does not contribute
significantly to the impact of your argument because it will,
instead, diminish it. Give me one or two good reasons to do
something and I will. When you promise 20, and the eleventh
sounds marginal, I am getting bored, I have forgotten the first
10, and I now assume they must all have been as lame as this
one. Paradoxically, more reasons create less persuasive force. In
the world of persuasion, less really is more.

Order your thoughts logically

The sequence in which you present your information matters.
You may have a long justification for your point of view, and you
may want me to hear it. But if you make me wait for your main
point, while you describe all of the stages of your thought process,
you run the risk that I will mentally switch off. The US Army has
it right with its injunction: BLUF – Bottom Line Up Front.

In the remainder of this chapter you will learn:

- how to BLUF with a powerful and repeatable process for hooking your audience, whether it is one person or a thousand, and whether it is in print or in person;
- how to sequence your ideas logically;
- how to close your argument elegantly.

The PPaP process for hooking your audience

The PPaP process sets out four steps that will hook your audience. It presents people with the three essential pieces of information they need before deciding whether to pay attention, and combines four powerful pieces of psychology.

The first of these pieces of psychology is the primacy effect on memory – the first piece of information we receive will stick in the mind. So will the last piece of information – the recency effect. This means that a powerful opening statement and a powerful closing statement are vital to influencing people.

The PPaP process harnesses the primacy effect extremely well. PPaP stands for:

- Position
- Pressure
- ask
- Point of view.

Each of the three Ps provides the person or people you want to influence with valuable information, preparing them to accept your argument.

Step 1: State the *position*

If you hit me with a powerful statement out of the blue, I may not be ready for it; so it may not fix properly in my memory.

If shock is your intent, you will achieve it, but you may want a more considered response from me. You need to make me comfortable.

Start by building rapport with me by telling me something uncontroversial that I can accept without resistance. This will set the context and allow my brain to access the right mental filing cabinet, so it is ready to store the information you are about to give me.

Step 2: Put me under some *pressure*

Too much agreeable background will allow me to relax more than you want. I will think "So what, I know all of this". The next step is to give me a reason to pay attention. So tell me why this matters to me. What is the problem, the pain, the pressure that you are going to address? If you raise the stakes for me, then I am compelled to hear you out.

Step 3: Now *ask* a question

What does a question do to the person who hears or reads it?

In your mind, you are starting to form an answer, so the first impact of a question is to engage your mind actively. It is reaching a peak of attention that will allow you to remember the key insight that is coming up.

The other thing a question does is create in your mind one or more answers. Better still for the questioner would be the realisation that you don't have an answer. Now you are at a peak of alertness. You want to compare your answer with mine or, if you have none, you want to find out what my answer is.

Once you have put me under pressure, pose a question. You can do this by asking one outright: "What is the next step?" or by implying one: "You may be wondering what the next step is."

Step 4: State your *point of view*

This is your bottom line, your key insight, the one thing that you want me to remember, consider and act on.

Does this pattern work?

Look at the opening paragraphs of several magazine articles; some will fit this pattern. Newspaper journalism often has a different format, but you will still find some examples of this sequence in the press. Some books even follow this structure.

▶ brilliant example

Position

It is a truth universally acknowledged that a single man in possession of a good fortune must be in want of a wife.

However little known the feelings or views of such a man may be on his first entering a neighbourhood, this truth is so well fixed in the minds of the surrounding families, that he is considered as the rightful property of some one or other of their daughters.

Pressure

"My dear Mr. Bennet," said his lady to him one day, "have you heard that Netherfield Park is let at last?"

Mr. Bennet replied that he had not.

"But it is," returned she; "for Mrs. Long has just been here, and she told me all about it."

Mr. Bennet made no answer.

ask

"Do not you want to know who has taken it?" cried his wife impatiently.

"You want to tell me, and I have no objection to hearing it."

This was invitation enough.

Point of view

"Why, my dear, you must know, Mrs. Long says that Netherfield is taken by a young man of large fortune from the north of England; that he came down on Monday in a chaise and four to see the place, and was so much delighted with it that he agreed with Mr. Morris immediately; that he is to take possession before Michaelmas, and some of his servants are to be in the house by the end of next week.

This is the opening of Jane Austen's *Pride and Prejudice*, and it has certainly compelled a fair number of readers to read on.

As you get more skilled with this sequence, you can vary it according to your needs:

- You can lead with your point of view, and then set it in the context of the position and pressure.
- You can begin with the pressure, to create a high impact opening.
- You can start with a question, to get your audience mentally engaged.

A logical structure for your argument

The fundamental question

Your argument addresses an implied question about your point of view. You may assert that something needs to be done, so your argument could address "how" to do it, or "why" you are right to say so.

The first thing to decide in structuring your argument is what question you want to address. You have two choices:

1 You can focus on the question *you* want to address.

2 You can focus on the question *I* want you to address

The second is the bolder and more powerful approach, but it is riskier, if you are not as well prepared. If you are lucky, both questions will be the same.

Having stated your point of view, the two most likely questions that will occur to your audience are "why?" and "how?" A generalisation that is often true is that more senior and powerful people will be more likely to focus on "why?" and more junior and technical people will want you to address "how?".

You can address both, of course. If you do so, address them one at a time, and start with "why?"

Addressing the "why?" question
If you choose to deal with "why?", you will need to give a series of reasons or justifications. Start with the most important reason, support it with evidence, and then move on to the next reason. Be mindful of the Pareto principle and limit yourself to a maximum three reasons.

brilliant tip

If you have a load more reasons, they are unlikely to sway your argument if the three main ones are unsuccessful. However, you may want to demonstrate that you have done the work, so do so with a statement like this:

"There are other reasons that I could give. They complement the three I have already discussed, but what you have already heard is already compelling."

Addressing the "how?" question
The commonest way to answer such a question is to present a logical sequence of steps: step 1, followed by supporting

information; then step 2, and so on. If there are too many steps (seven is a good maximum to work to) then reduce them by dividing the process into phases, each with a number of steps:

- *Phase A* – Step 1, Step 2, Step 3;
- *Phase B* – Step 4, Step 5, Step 6, Step 7;
- *Phase C* – Step 8, Step 9, Step 10.

Other ways to organise your arguments

If a series of reasons in priority order or a sequence of steps does not suit the information you need to give, look for another logical sequence to use. Here are a few examples:

- Structural – e.g. departments of an organisation, geographical regions, components of a manufactured item;
- Functional – e.g. job roles, building trades, parts of the body;
- Classification – e.g. types of animal, book subjects, vehicle types;
- Sequential – e.g. time (forwards or backwards), scale (big to small, or vice versa), distance (nearest to furthest, or vice versa).

How many parts?

We have seen that less is more; is there a magic number? Unfortunately, there are several candidates.

Magic number seven

George Miller referred to seven as a magic number at the end of a series of tests, which included asking people to remember a series of words or numbers. He found that the average number that people could reliably recall 50% or more of the time was seven. If you have more than seven things in your list, few people will remember all of them.

Magic number five

Whilst the average number of things that most people can hold in their memory is seven, we are all different – as are circumstances. Miller found that the number of items ranged from five to nine: so he referred to "The magic number seven, plus or minus two". Since you won't want to presume all of your audience has the maximum capacity, it is safer to assume the opposite. A good working number of items to include in your list for maximum recall-ability is five.

Magic number four

"Subitising" refers to our ability to recognise how many objects are in a collection without counting them. For most people, we can subitise one, two, three or four objects. If there are more, we have to count them quickly to know how many there are. This suggests that four components or fewer – particularly in a diagram – will have greater impact than five or more.

Magic number three

In the next chapter, you will learn about creating powerful speech patterns. When you listen to great speakers, you will often notice lists of three things. This has worked its way into Western speech rhythms and into popular cliché, from wine, women and song to Tom, Dick and Harry.

brilliant tip

People love checklists. By including a checklist, you signal that you have lots of information, and that your thinking is complete.

Anticipate "what if?"

To make your case truly influential, you have to demonstrate that you can think flexibly and have anticipated a range of

demonstrate that you
can think flexibly and
have anticipated a
range of future scenarios

future scenarios; not just the one you are promoting. Present the risks and obstacles to your proposition. This will have two effects. First, it shows that you are aware of the problems and gives you a chance to demonstrate the answers you have: how you would mitigate the risks and what contingency plans you could recommend.

Second, if I spot a risk, my instinct will be to reject your proposal. I will feel you are pushing me to do something that could go wrong and will push back against it. If you point out the risk, I will feel as if you have restored my choices and I can be more objective in weighing my options.

Seize your last opportunity

Earlier, you saw that the primacy and the recency effects each assist the impact of what you say, by helping make parts of it more memorable. Your last opportunity to have an impact on me and make your proposition memorable is with your closing remarks.

Too often, people fail to prepare this part of their pitch. They end poorly and, at best, miss the chance to boost their influence. At worst, they steal some of their own impact. Here is a list of seven great ways to end a spoken or written presentation of an idea or proposal.

1   *Summary and clincher.* Summarise your main points and conclude with "Therefore ..." or "So ...".

2   *No-brainer.* Takes the form: "You want to ... I've shown you how you can. You do want to ... *don't you?*"

3   *Close the drawer.* At the start of your piece, start a relevant story that illustrates your argument. At the close, finish the story, giving a satisfying sense of completion.

4   *Conditional ending.* Takes the form: "If you . . . then you will get . . ."

5   *Visualise the outcome.* Describe an enticing future that is the result of the action you have advocated. Alternatively, you might visualise a bleak future if they don't. For maximum power, try the contrast of "If you don't . . . but if you do . . ."

6   *The personal touch.* Close by translating the abstract arguments you have made into a compelling human example.

7   *Call to action.* Enumerate the next steps (three maximum, please) that you want the person to take.

brilliant recap

- People need a reason to act or change their thinking – always give a compelling "because".
- Dodgy data will undermine your case. Check your facts and get your logic right.
- BLUF: Bottom Line Up Front.
- An enticing introduction contains a context-setting position statement, an alertness-raising pressure statement, a brain-engaging question (ask), and an insightful point of view: PPaP.
- Structure your main argument logically, so that the flow of your information is easy to follow, thus easy to agree with.
- Close strongly to increase your influence.

CHAPTER 6

The power of how you say it

Have you ever made a compelling case for something and been right? And known you were right? And had a sound logical reason why you were right? And even had a mountain of good hard evidence to show you were right? Yet despite all this, you were still unable to persuade the other person?

Of course you have; we all have. The reason for this is the big E: emotion. Emotion is why we do things. Most decisions are really made on emotional grounds; we just use logic and evidence to justify them.

> most decisions are really made on emotional grounds; we just use logic and evidence to justify them

This chapter investigates how to use your language to tap into people's emotions. This means three things: inspiring enthusiasm, framing the proposition and using language that connects you to your listener.

Inspire

When reason is not enough, you must inspire. When you can get people to feel emotions, they are far easier to influence. When we feel a strong emotion, we become less analytical; it is almost as if the blood flowing to the emotional centre of our brain has been diverted from the logical part.

The particular bit of our thinking that is compromised concerns assessment of scale. So, when we are scared by a public health threat, the fear leads us irrationally to discount the scale of the problem. A dreaded disease affecting three people will cause almost as much concern as one affecting 3,000.

On the other hand, say you are a painter and decorator and are discussing how much work is needed in my house: by conjuring up how good my family and I will feel when you have repainted the walls *and* the woodwork in my lounge and, while you are here, how much we'll love it if the hall is repainted and feeling fresh and homely ... now I am starting to be compelled by the emotion. Consequently, the difference in price will seem less than if you had just given me the additional price quote.

Visualising the future

Getting an emotional response requires that you make the situation real for people. You need to conjure up imagery and physical sensations with your language. This means working hard to use simple language, rooted in the physical senses. This may sound easy; it is not. This is especially true in these days of corporate-style management-speak.

---

brilliant example

The following is an example of a worthy vision that corporate executives might have for their organisation:

"I have a vision of an ethnic diversity where everybody has full equality of opportunity and where we can harness the synergies of a multi-ethnic workforce, collaborating to construct an enhanced community."

We sort of know what this means, and it sounds good. What would happen if we allowed ourselves to use everyday language and to use that language to paint vivid pictures? Here is an alternative version:

"I have a dream that one day on the red hills of Georgia the sons of former slaves and the sons of former slave owners will be able *to sit down together at the table of brotherhood*.

I have a dream that one day even the state of Mississippi, a state *sweltering with the heat of injustice, sweltering with the heat of oppression*, will be transformed into *an oasis of freedom and justice*.

I have a dream that *my four little children* will one day live in a nation where they will not be judged by the color of their skin but by the content of their character. I have a dream today!

I have a dream that one day, down in Alabama, with its vicious racists, with its governor having his lips dripping with the words of interposition and nullification; one day right there in Alabama *little black boys and black girls will be able to join hands with little white boys and white girls* as sisters and brothers. I have a dream today!"

The above example is, of course, the words of Dr Martin Luther King Junior, with my emphasis. In those phrases, Dr King creates descriptions that leave impressions that stick. "Sweltering in the heat of injustice" turns an abstract concept into a physical experience. This is genius-level influencing, but the principle is available to us all.

How to create images

The English language offers you three main ways to create images for your audience or readers. Let's take a brief look at each.

Simile

A simile is a brief statement that one thing is like another. Usually, it compares something big and complex to something much smaller and simpler, as in the movie *Forrest Gump*:

"Life is like a box of chocolates ..."

It sets up an image in our mind that has more power than a direct explanation. When the relevance of the image is not obvious, it also allows you to explain the meaning and set up a memorable "aha" moment. Forrest Gump continues:

"... you never know what you are going to get."

Similes are therefore at their most powerful when the listener has to work hard to find the connection. If I state that:

"Influence is like a tree ..."

You can find a number of possible reasons. I am letting you do the work, so you will make my point for me. Once you have done the work, I can then put my point of view:

"... because the more roots it grows, the stronger it becomes."

At the opposite extreme, beware of clichés. They have little or no power to influence and can become a source of sarcastic amusement. How many athletes can "run like the wind"?

Metaphor

Metaphors have more power than similes because they are stated more confidently. Instead of "influence is like a tree", a metaphor would actually equate the two: "influence is a tree".

At their best, metaphors become the new names for things that are hard to describe, like Churchill's "iron curtain" or Robert Frost's "road not taken".

Part of the power of Dr King's speech is in the number of metaphors. In the four paragraphs above, there are ten metaphors and only one simile. It gets more power because four of the metaphors are repeated; one of them six times.

Analogy, parable, allegory

These three things all draw an extended comparison between one thing and another. Parables and allegories take the form of a story, where the subject of the story represents a more abstract or personal idea. The term "parable" tends to describe narratives that are designed to teach a moral or religious point, whilst "allegories" are more widely used to draw political or social comparisons.

When we hear a series of metaphors and similes in a consistent way, the speaker is building up an analogy. For example, "Influence is like a tree and where each root touches something, it persuades. The roots are nourished by the ideas they soak up from the soil." As this example starts to show, if you try to sustain an analogy for too long it starts to get weaker and appear absurd.

In all these cases, you are using one thing, which your audience can readily relate to from their everyday experience, to symbolise another, more complex, idea.

brilliant tip

Names have tremendous power to influence. When Churchill used the expression "iron curtain", he was not just using a metaphor; he was naming something. Naming a concept makes it easier to talk about – and therefore easier to spread the idea. It also gives something a reality. So, to make your idea, proposal or project more influential, name it. When you name something, here are a few tips:

- *Be alert for unintended alternative interpretations.* The authority of your idea can easily be undermined if its name can be understood in a different way. The name of the Babel Project may be intended to convey a grand vision of people working together, but to some it conveyed hubris and a project that would ultimately fail.

- *Use a word that is easy to pronounce.* People are loath to talk about something they cannot pronounce, in case they get it wrong.

- *If the name has more than one word, check out the acronym.*
  The Social Housing Investment Trust would sound great until
  people get fed up with writing the full name and revert to its
  initials.

Tell stories

Human beings are storytelling creatures; deep in our history,
we started to gather around campfires and listen to stories. The

power of narrative continues to grip
us. You only have to consider the
popularity of soap operas and celebrity gossip to recognise that a good
story hooks an audience.

**human beings are
storytelling creatures**

When politicians want to make a point, the best communicators
among them rarely start with statistics or philosophical analysis;
instead, they tell us a story. The impact of a distant disaster
may be in the tens of thousands, but the charities that need our
money to save or rebuild lives will invariably tell us the story of
one family, or one mother, or one orphaned child.

To influence an audience, use a story built from a relevant
example to hook them and make your principal point. When you
do this, you combine the power of storytelling to hook attention
with the power of emotion to reduce critical evaluation.

 **brilliant** example

I could tell you that there is more to making a sale than knowing the facts
and figures. Or, I could tell you a short story:

"I remember it was a very cold morning. I got to my potential client's
office early, because this may have been the most important meeting

of my career to date. As I walked to the offices, I knew I had prepared well for the meeting. I'd been almost obsessive. I'd stayed up late, and then I'd got up early and gone through it again. I was at the start of my career, and an expert in our methodology; I had studied the client's documents; I was eager to impress. This opportunity was a big deal for our firm.

So, how'd it go? I bombed. Crashed, burned, and left with scars. It was probably embarrassing, but I was too shaken to be sure."

Looking back, there was nothing wrong with my technical preparation. Unfortunately, I knew next to nothing about how to handle a sales situation. I learned something very important, that changed my professional life: no amount of technical skill and expertise will be enough, on its own, to build lasting, profitable client relationships, and sell valuable business products and services.

Be specific

So, telling stories hooks attention and triggers emotions. Human stories also work for another reason: the power of the particular. Somehow a story about Mrs K's little girl is more believable than the seemingly abstract plight of 10,000 thousand children. One little girl seems real to us, whilst 10,000 are a statistic. Specific language makes it easier for us to imagine the situation and put ourselves into it. Because it triggers empathy, the situation becomes a part of our consciousness; because we've identified a single person, we cannot escape the truth of it; because we feel strongly, we immediately believe it – the strength of feeling conveys a sense of reality to us.

Being specific makes your statements more believable. Compare these two examples:

1   Scientists have found that how we present a situation influences how other people perceive it.

2   Two psychologists, Amos Tversky and Daniel Kahneman, have found three ways that the description of a situation can affect the way I will perceive it.

The first is weaker. It allows you, the reader, to make your own interpretations and question the assertion. Who are these scientists, what are their qualifications, how much influence, and who will be influenced?

In the second statement, you cannot deny these are real scientists because I have named them. You know they study psychology and, knowing that there are three ways that they have found, the possibility of influence becomes more real. You also know that they can work for *you* when you are trying to influence *me*.

Seven ways to be more specific
The following approaches will keep your argument specific:

1   Name names.

2   Quote examples.

3   Describe processes.

4   Use numbered lists.

5   Use numbers and statistics.

6   Give baselines for comparisons.

7   Avoid words like "could", "might", "can" or "may".

Frame

"Frames" are the way you surround your topic with an introduction or context that will affect how people assess it.

Two psychologists, Amos Tversky and Daniel Kahneman, have found three ways that the description of a situation can affect the way I will perceive it: through anchoring, ease of recall and familiarity. Their work revealed more about how we make judgements when we feel some uncertainty. I have described these as "dangerous frames" because they introduce a bias which interferes with careful, analytical thought.

Dangerous frames

Your brain is not entirely under your control and sometimes makes judgements based on irrelevant or peripheral information. This can lead you into mistakes and offers influencers ways to manipulate you. Never is this more surprising than with anchoring.

Anchoring

Ethiopia published its population in July 2008 as 79,221,000. Malaysia published its population in 2009. What is the population of Malaysia?

Make an estimate or have a guess.

If you have a response, answer a second question: what is the relevance of Ethiopia's population to your estimate of Malaysia's population?

The answer to the second question is "none". Yet most of us will find our answer to Malaysia's population is heavily influenced by the number 79,221,000. If the first information I'd given you was the population of Greece, at 11,306,183 in January 2010, most people's answer would almost certainly have been a lower number for the population of Malaysia. Unless, that is, you already had a good idea of Malaysia's population.

Hearing a number, even an irrelevant one, before a question will influence your answer. This is because, in the absence of any other information, it creates a benchmark in your mind: an anchor. Tversky and Kahneman conducted many experiments.

The answer, by the way, is 28,306,700 – but don't worry if your own estimate was much higher.

▶ brilliant example

Tversky and Kahneman asked two groups of high school students to estimate the answer to a sum in 5 seconds – not enough time to calculate an answer.

Group A had to estimate: $8 \times 7 \times 6 \times 5 \times 4 \times 3 \times 2 \times 1$

Group B had to estimate: $1 \times 2 \times 3 \times 4 \times 5 \times 6 \times 7 \times 8$

Looking at the average answers, they found that both groups underestimated the true answer (40,320) but that more of Group B had underestimated the answer, and by a bigger amount, than Group A. The first numbers that Group B saw were 1 and 2. Group A first saw 8 and 7.

Ease of recall

When something has happened recently, or when we have an example to hand, it has more power to influence our judgements. People mistrust train transport more after an accident has been in the news and take out more insurance after a natural disaster like flooding. By reminding people of relevant examples, you strengthen the argument you are making.

Familiarity

Linda studied ecology at university and is deeply concerned about the environment. She wears a lot of second-hand clothes at the weekend and rides a bike. She does not own a car. Which of these is more likely?

a   Linda has a senior post in a bank.

b   Linda has a senior post in a bank and is an active member of an environmental campaign group.

If you picked (b) then you are probably in the majority. When Kahneman and Tversky asked a similar question, 85% chose the answer like (b). In fact, since the two things are unrelated, (a) is more likely – if 100 Lindas held senior posts in a bank, then probably not all of them would be active in a campaign group.

People pick (b) because there is a narrative that fits a familiar pattern. When we encounter a story that makes sense, we are more likely to believe it than simply a blind chance.

This is one reason (there are others) why so many people connected autism with the MMR vaccine in the UK. Statistically, some children who are autistic will show the first symptoms near to the time of an early childhood vaccine. But coincidence makes a poor story. One thing causing the other makes some sense out of a tragedy.

To use this bias with integrity, you need to create an honest story that illustrates your point.

Win or lose

There is a second reason why people were willing to stop their children from having a life-saving vaccine in the UK (measles is a killer). It seems that people are more incentivised to protect themselves against a loss than to secure a gain.

A £1 lottery ticket has a statistical value of 50 pence. For every £100 of tickets bought, £50 goes into the prize fund and the rest goes to administration, good causes and profit for the operators and their agents.

So if you buy a ticket for £1, and I then offer to buy it back, how much would you accept? Rationally, you should accept 51 pence but few would. Few would even accept £1. In the back of your mind, that ticket could be worth £1,000 or even £1 million. And the fear of losing that would outweigh the benefit of a small gain compared to the amount you would expect to get statistically.

 **example**

This goes even deeper than fear of losing a big win. We are reluctant to give up what we have. In the United States, two states took measures to reduce legal action following road traffic accidents. New Jersey and Pennsylvania adopted two different schemes to reduce court action. On the face of it, both would achieve the same effect. In fact, the results were very different.

New Jersey
Under the new legislation, drivers automatically get limited rights to sue as part of their insurance policy, but with an option to buy extended rights to sue.

What proportion opted for cheaper policy and limited rights?

Pennsylvania
Under the new legislation, drivers automatically get full rights to sue as part of their insurance policy, but with an option to accept limitation and lower premiums.

What proportion opted for cheaper policy and limited rights?

In New Jersey, 80% of drivers chose to stick with the cheaper policy. The scheme was a success. In Pennsylvania, only 25% of drivers chose to give up some of their rights to sue, to save money on their policy.

Positive frames

In Chapter 5, you saw the PPaP approach to introducing an idea, a proposal, a talk or a report. The first P in PPaP is position and a powerful way to establish your position is to set a positive frame around what you are about to say. Here are 12 positive frames you can set: four that are useful in making progress, three for generating new ideas, and five for reviewing what you have.

Making progress

1 *Agreement frame.* Establish right from the outset that you are in fundamental agreement. This can pave the way for introducing a variant point of view, focused on a detail: "You say my report isn't good enough. I agree ... and ..."

2 *Outcome frame.* Set the discussion as a search for a shared goal or target. Once you have a shared outcome, the process of working together and securing agreement becomes far easier:

"Let's discuss what we want to achieve."

3 *Solution frame.* Focus the conversation on finding solutions that satisfy the constraints. In problem solving a powerful way to unstick people focused on the problem is to re-state the problem as a solution:

"If we are going to raise the money we want to, the solution will be how to ..."

4 *Action frame.* Create a plan that will get things done. Breaking a job into manageable steps and allocating those steps fairly among a team makes it easier for everyone to contribute and get things done:

"Let's allocate responsibilities and set some deadlines."

New ideas

5 *"What if?" frame.* Create options by assuming some obstacles could be removed. "What if?" gives you the option to remove the problem temporarily from the real world with an imagined "fix", find a solution, and then revert to the new problem of how to make the fix:

"We need more space. What would happen if we already had the space, but were using it for something unimportant?"

6 *Creativity frame.* Give permission to make suggestions that are wild and provocative. The most important criterion for encouraging true creativity is to remove any sanctions or penalties for being wrong:

"It is OK to suggest anything – we will suspend judgement at this stage."

7 *Playful frame.* The most creative people in the world are children. They make no assumptions about what is and is not possible and they test every boundary. Enhance creativity by inviting people into that child-like state:

"Let us play with the ideas, say whatever we want and experiment."

Reviewing

8 *Process frame.* When conversations get sticky, you can never go wrong by stepping back and reverting to a process for resolving the problem. If you cannot agree on an idea, agree on a process to review the idea:

"Let's look at how to proceed from here and find a common approach."

9 *Evidence frame.* Evidence is one of your most powerful tools as an influencer. The evidence frame establishes that the conversation is about what evidence is relevant, what is available, and how to evaluate the evidence:

"The next thing to focus on is evidence; let's start by listing what we need and what we have."

10 *Critical frame.* Pre-empt criticism by introducing it yourself. If you do this, you are showing a willingness to be tested, and a recognition that few ideas are without compromises and faults. By exposing the criticisms, you have a chance to deal with them yourself:

"Let's turn to the potential shortcomings of this idea."

11 *Emotional frame.* No decision will ever be made without at least an element of emotion. So introduce this explicitly, so that all parties recognise the part emotion is playing:

"So, how do you feel about this subject . . .?"

12 *Intuitive frame.* In areas where people have real expertise – not least when a decision is about themselves – intuition is a powerful source of information that can lead to a reliable decision, even if we cannot articulate why:

"So, how do you feel about this subject . . .?"

Connect

Adapting the immortal words of Ella Fitzgerald (written by jazz musicians Melvin "Sy" Oliver and James "Trummy" Young): "It ain't what you say, it's the way that you say it."

brilliant example

Try saying this aloud:

"I never said she stole the money."

Whatever this sounds like it means, you can change the meaning entirely, by changing the word that you stress. Try repeating it out loud, but stressing the word that is underlined:

"<u>I</u> never said she stole the money."

"I <u>never</u> said she stole the money."

"I never <u>said</u> she stole the money."

"I never said <u>she</u> stole the money."

"I never said she <u>stole</u> the money."

"I never said she stole the <u>money</u>."

The way you say things matters. For thousands of years, people have been perfecting the art of rhetoric: how to use language effectively. Much of what orators like politicians and professional speakers learn today was first codified by the ancient Greeks and perfected by the Romans. Consequently, the ideas can feel complex and alien to us. They are not. Whenever you hear a great speaker – whether a recording of Dr Martin Luther King or a modern day speech by Barack Obama, whether a nation-defining political speech by Winston Churchill or a technology-defining commercial presentation by Steve Jobs – the way they deliver their message uses simple techniques that you too can learn and deploy.

Keeping it simple

 **tip**

KISS – Keep It Short & Simple.

KISS is one of the most often cited pieces of advice for a communicator. But what does it mean? The best communication has maximum impact on the listener or reader; and it has that impact quickly. Short and simple language penetrates our brains rapidly and accurately. Many of the techniques of rhetoric work because they offer shortcuts into our consciousness.

The five-year-old test

If you want to communicate powerfully, a brilliant test of your language is this: what would a five-year-old make of it? As adults, we can recognise lots of big and complicated words, and we can unscramble long and complex sentences. But doing so takes effort; in computer language, it takes processing power. "Short and simple" requires less work – it penetrates the clever outer layers of our adult brain and ends up at the inside child brain, where we instantly understand it.

Take a selection of newspapers and magazines from your local newsagent. Which have the more skilled communicators: *The Observer*, *The Times*, *New Statesman* and *New Scientist*, or *The Sun*, *Daily Mirror*, *Hello* and *FHM*? Ignoring the merits of the content and your own personal preferences, which set can be read by more people? Getting your message across simply is a skill, but of course having a powerful message is equally important. If you can do both, then you have the power to influence.

The influence equation

We can summarise this into a simple equation:

The impact of your message =
the quality of your message/the effort required to understand it.

Keep it positive

If I tell you not to think about what you are going to do tomorrow, what creeps into your mind? It is the clever, grown-up bit of your brain that has to figure out the meaning of logical words like "not", "don't", "either", "neither", "must", "could", "should" and "cannot". The quick and powerful communication comes from "real" words: nouns, which describe things, and verbs, which describe actions. Use these words to carry the meaning of what you want to say.

The power of "but"

"You have done a wonderful job but ..."

As soon as we hear the word "but", our brains prepare for the truth. We immediately discount the words that have gone before and think to ourselves, "Aha, here comes the truth".

So, be very careful with your use of the word "but" – and its more sophisticated cousins: "although", "yet" and "however". They have the power to destroy an important part of your message. You will usually be able to rephrase what you wanted to say using the word "and" instead: "You have done a wonderful job, and ..."

Tapping into my thinking style

In Chapter 2, you read how you can build rapport by spotting other people's preferences for "seeing" words, "hearing" words, "doing" words and "logical" words. This is one way to tap into their preferred thinking styles and influence their thinking more effectively. There are other ways that people think, which you can notice and match, to get your message across more powerfully.

Big picture or small detail?
Some people want to understand your message in its widest context and are not really interested in specific details. They are "big picture" people who like grand ideas and want to understand the deeper meaning of the ideas you are promoting. The question "why?" is important to them because it directs them towards purpose.

Other people may focus on the details; they like mechanisms, facts and data. If you talk in generalities, they will be frustrated by your unwillingness to get down to specifics. They need you to describe the "how" of things before they will be prepared to trust you.

Logic or feelings?
There are two fundamentally different approaches that people will take to making decisions. Some will focus on impersonal logic and make decisions with their head. To them, "the truth" is essential; more so than tact. If something is not expressed logically or is unsupported by the facts, it will literally not make sense to them and they will reject it absolutely.

Facts and logic are far less important to others, however. They prefer to focus on people and values, and make their decisions with their heart. To them, harmony is more important than some abstract "truth". They want to deal with people compassionately, and value feelings as much as facts.

Always remember that whichever of these two I may prioritise, my own emotional response to a situation will be an important determinant in the way I assess your message. If you want to influence me, you may not choose to appeal to other people's emotions, but you must always appeal to mine.

The need for persistence

Some people automatically "get it" as soon as you have made your point. Others need the chance to dwell on your ideas for some time before they get it. Some even need to go over the same ground again and again before they convince themselves of the point you have made. Powerful rhetoric gives you a way to repeat ideas for the people who need it, in such a way that those who "got it" quickly do not perceive you as patronising them.

On a one-to-one basis, you should be constantly checking levels of understanding and responding with new information or restating what you have already said, according to the response you get.

Power speech

In a memorable episode of the popular television series, *The West Wing*, "Somebody's Going to Emergency, Somebody's Going to Jail", the character of Toby Ziegler, portrayed by Richard Schiff, refers to the science of listener attention. He shows how speech-writers use repetition, opposites and a climax, or surprise ending, to create a powerful effect.

This science goes back to the ancient Greeks, who called it rhetoric, codified it, and taught it in their academies. Political speech-writers are masters of rhetoric, using the patterns and rhythms of language to grab and hold attention, to emphasise ideas, and make them memorable. Following a few simple processes, you can do the same.

Repetition

There are many ways to use repetition for effect. We might think of a farmer extolling the virtues of organic produce: "Carrots are tastier, tomatoes are tastier, beans are tastier, apples are tastier, free-range eggs are tastier."

Here, each item in his list ends with the same word. Alternatively, he could have started with the same words: "Tastier carrots, tastier tomatoes, tastier beans, tastier apples, tastier free-range eggs." Notice also how he has omitted the normal "and" that would have preceded the last item on his list, to give the effect of a long and powerful list. He could also have achieved a similar effect by the repetition of "and" between each item: "Carrots are tastier and tomatoes are tastier and beans are tastier and apples are tastier and free-range eggs are tastier."

Our farmer could simply have repeated a key word: "Carrots are tastier; everything is tastier" or used his repetition to amplify his meaning: "Everything is tastier; tastier in every meal." He could have repeated the idea of tastier by using alternative words: "Everything is tastier, less bland, more flavoursome." Each of these creates emphasis and rhythm, making the words more powerful.

There are lots more ways he could have used repetition. He could repeat the first word of one phrase as the last word of the next: "Tastier vegetables, and meat that is tastier" or the opposite, starting the second phrase with the last word of the first: "Vegetables are tastier, and tastier meat."

Another way you can create emphasis is by repeating sound. The three common ways to do this in English are to repeat the starting sound: "Tastier peaches, pears and plums"; to repeat the ending sound: "Tastier swedes, peas and cheese"; and to repeat the overall sound of the words: "Tastier leeks, beans and peas."

As a final example, taking a lead from former British Prime Minister Tony Blair's famous "Education, education, education", our farmer could have said: "Everything is tastier, tastier, tastier."

Which of these examples is best? Often it will be a matter of personal preference and the need not to overdo the effect.

The power of threes

Simply putting together a list is a powerful rhetorical technique, but speakers and writers can emphasise that list by putting together precisely three items – three words, three phrases or three sentences. Something about the rhythm this creates makes a triplet sound good to us.

It also seems to sound best if the one element that differs or is longer comes at the end: "... life, liberty, and the American way."

The emotional power of lists of three is so great that even when lists of four are used, we typically remember only three.

▶ brilliant example

One of Sir Winston Churchill's speeches is often misquoted. What he said:

"I have nothing to offer but blood, toil, tears and sweat"

is often mis-quoted as:

"I have nothing to offer but blood, sweat and tears".

Not just the power of threes, but the importance of the sound of words one against the other. Churchill's skill with language was phenomenal, so why did he use a flawed line? In fact, he was quoting a line spoken by US President Theodore Roosevelt, 43 years earlier.

Opposites

In our example, our farmer might say of organic farming: "It reduces toxins: it increases flavour." Reduces and increases are opposites, which he sets against one another. Here are three more ways to do this: three Cs.

- *Contradiction.* The farmer could, for example, have said: "I don't say it increases toxins; I say it reduces them."
- *Contrast.* The farmer could have contrasted organic methods with chemicals: "Organic farming reduces toxins; chemicals increase them."
- *Comparison.* The farmer could have compared the effects of organic methods and chemicals: "Organic farming reduces toxicity more than chemicals increase yields."

All these examples have a "this not that" structure that is responsible for some of the most memorable phrases we have, like Neil Armstrong's "One small step for a man; one giant leap for mankind".

Climax

Our farmer has used a repeating list to build expectation, then a pair of opposites to heighten the tension. He will now cap it all. This structure of increasing power is called a climax (from the Latin word for ladder, and linked to our word, climb).

He could, for example, use a blunt statement with no rhetorical flourish to create real contrast, and use content that is also very different; not about farming matters, as the earlier parts are, but about economics: "Organic food is sustainable."

"Carrots are tastier, tomatoes are tastier, beans are tastier, apples are tastier, free-range eggs are tastier. Organic farming reduces toxins: it increases flavour. Organic food is sustainable."

Questions and answers

One way to command attention from an audience is to ask questions. If you ask a question in a presentation or in text, you have two choices. What are they?

You could tell your reader or audience the answer, or you could leave the question unanswered; a rhetorical question, such as: "How could anybody oppose organic food?"

If you do choose to answer, you can use your question to introduce the next part of your argument, or to deal with a question or objection that you are anticipating: "Some would ask, 'How can organic food be more sustainable?' I will answer that question."

Over- and understatement

Deliberate overstatement, sometimes called hyperbole, is used a million times a day by school children. To be effective, it must either be witty or it must avoid being so overstated that it draws attention to itself, rather than the point you want to make. If the latter happens, then the hyperbole becomes a source of ridicule.

Whilst our farmer might have said, "Carrots are tastier, tomatoes are tastier, beans are tastier, apples are tastier, free-range eggs are tastier, hundreds of things are tastier", it is unlikely to have had a positive effect if there were a gross exaggeration: "Carrots are tastier, tomatoes are tastier, beans are tastier, apples are tastier, free-range eggs are tastier, millions of things are tastier."

A particularly British speech pattern is to do the opposite, and understate things for effect: "For people who want to live healthier lives, better food is worth having." Indeed, the British are so fond of dramatic understatement that they sometimes turn a statement on its head: "For people who want to live healthier lives, better food is no bad thing."

Power words

Having learned how to combine words using the art of rhetoric, the last choice to make is which words to use. Some words do carry greater power than others. Using them effectively can enhance the influencing power of what you say. The list of examples below contains words that are frequently used in successful advertising and marketing.

⌐ `brilliant` impact

Power words

Because	Discover/Learn
You/Your	Know/Understand
Please/Thank you	Create
Easy/Simple	Vital/Essential
Now/Today	Trust
Immediately	Powerful
Free	Help/Assistance
Save	Guaranteed
Safe/Protect	Best/Better
Health	Improved
Proven/Tested	Research

Names

There is one more word that has enormous power. For each person, their name is a power word. Use it from time to time in a conversation and they will feel special. If, on the other hand, you overuse their name, you will sound phoney – like poorly trained shop or call centre staff.

The other vital thing to remember when using my name is to use it properly. If I introduce myself to you as Mike, then call me Mike: not Michael, Mickey, Mick or Mikey. Any one of these may cause offence or make me uncomfortable. Many people who use a contraction of a name (like Mike for Michael) will only use the full name in a family context. When you call me Michael, you remind me of my mum. Since you are not my mum, it sounds patronising. Other people use only the full version of their name. Contracting it may sound overfamiliar or just plain rude.

When you use names in print, make sure you get the spelling correct. This is especially the case with names from a different culture, or names which have a range of different spellings, such as Graeme or Graham, Briony or Bryony.

If you see a name in writing before you hear it, particularly a name from a different language or culture to your own, do ask how to pronounce it properly. Most people will be glad you care enough to get it right, rather than dismissive of your ignorance. When you hear them say their name, repeat it back to them to check you have it right, and then take care to get it right again and again.

Puny words
Some words will diminish the impact of your message, by hinting at doubt. If you can, avoid using them.

 **impact**

Puny words

Maybe	Suppose
Perhaps	Possible
Might	May
Could	

Finally, when you are speaking, one class of words will really steal your influence from you. We find articulate speech particularly persuasive, so the more you fill your speech with "ums" and "ers", the weaker you sound. One or two examples are natural, but if you do it too often, they will become noticeable and will raise unconscious doubts about your confidence in what you are saying.

This class of influence stealers also includes whole phrases, which mean nothing, but signal self doubt: "You know what I mean" suggests that I don't. "Isn't it?" suggests I need your confirmation to convince me, and "I mean" tagged on to the end of a statement suggests I am trying to persuade myself.

 **example**

For a great example of the power of words, take a look at this video: www.tinyurl.com/brilliantvideo

brilliant recap

● Inspire a vision of what you are saying with simple and vivid language that summons up images and emotions.

● Human beings love stories, so create a narrative structure to put your message across compellingly.

● Specific language is far more persuasive than generalities.

● How you frame your ideas or proposals can have a big impact on how they are perceived.

● String your words together using powerful patterns like repetition in threes, creating contrasts, and asking questions.

PART 3

Strategies

CHAPTER 7

Focus on the
question:
"What's in it
for me?"

The easiest way to influence somebody to do something is to ask them to do something that they already want to do. If this sounds obvious, it is. Self-interest is the most important motivator we have, so to ignore it as a source of influence would be foolish.

Your challenge as an influencer is to discover what is in my interest; to ask, "What's in it for me?" When you can find a way to link your objectives with mine and offer me an opportunity to satisfy my self-interest, then you have my support at your disposal. This chapter examines what makes up self-interest, how you can discover it, and what is the role of altruism – our desire to put other people's interests ahead of our own.

 **example**

FAB: Features – Advantages – Benefits

For sales people, understanding self-interest is a vital part of the sales process. Having found out what the customer needs, your next step is to demonstrate the capability of the product or service you want to sell. There are three levels of capabilities: features, advantages and benefits.

- Features are the facts and figures about the product or service.
- Advantages make the product or service better than alternatives.

- Benefits meet the customer's needs, solve their problems and satisfy their self-interest.

Demonstrating benefits is the route to sales success.

What is self-interest?

What's in it for me? Self-interest is about getting what I want, whilst offering the minimum in return. On the surface, this is about things like better goods for lower prices, an easier work-load for higher pay, or my choice of holiday, when I want it.

A wide range of psychologists and thinkers have analysed self-interest to find out what motivates us. It is worth surveying their thinking, to understand the different levels of self-interest, and how to appeal to them.

We will look at four levels of self-interest: desires, needs, beliefs and values; and see how you can appeal to each in different ways.

Desires

Desires are the most superficial level of self-interest. They are the things that I want. They tend to be transient and, if you can fulfil my desires, then I will place huge value on this.

Influencers need to be aware of the boundary between needs and desires. You may perceive my needs as desires, but I may feel them as needs. The more of our needs that we fulfil, the greater priority we place on our desires, until they too become needs. It takes a very great spirit to say "I have enough" – most of us start to need things we never needed before, as we acquire more.

Needs

Needs are things that we perceive that we cannot do without. Abraham Maslow studied needs and concluded that they sit in a hierarchy of levels and once we meet one need, we feel a stronger need for other needs at the level above. Whilst his analysis is simplistic and we can feel different needs at the same time, the general observation matches our experience that some needs, like warmth, shelter and food, are more fundamental than others, such as status and fulfilment.

The important thing about needs is that meeting my needs is a shortcut to influence. So here is a list of human needs, collated from the work of a great many thinkers:

- need for survival (survival today);
- need for security (survival tomorrow);
- need for stimulation;
- need for social relationships and community;
- need for understanding of what is required from me;
- need for respect and authority;
- need for a sense of achievement;
- need for leisure;
- need for freedom to do what I want;
- need for growth;
- need to make a contribution.

If you can discover which of these needs dominate my attention and how I express those needs, then you can influence me by addressing those needs.

▶ brilliant example

You want volunteers to run in a charity sports event.

- **Francis** feels frustrated, because he never seems to get everything done, which leads to him working at weekends. He is not able to meet his need for achievement, so in trying to do so, he is compromising his need for leisure.

- *Approach*: Emphasise how training will give Francis more energy to get things done, and how he will enjoy the training activity as a leisure pursuit.

- **Leigh** has moved to a new area to take up an exciting new job. She is working long hours, to avoid going home and feeling alone. She is taking her mind off her need for social relationships by focusing too much on her work.

- *Approach*: Stress to Leigh how many new people she can meet as she prepares, and the social opportunities that will arise.

Beliefs

We have beliefs about everything and many of these are carried for a long time without challenge.

It is easy to influence me to do something that is consistent with my beliefs. Getting me to do something which conflicts with my beliefs requires that you first change the belief or, at the very least, shake it up enough.

It is election time and, for example, if I believe that "all politicians are on the make, in it only for themselves and that one lot are very much the same as the other", then persuading me to vote is going to be a tough job. But this is what you set out to do.

The path of least resistance

The easy route is to influence my thinking in a way that is consistent with this belief, without challenging it. Here are a couple of tactics:

- If politicians are pretty much the same, why not look for one small difference and vote for the candidate that is a tiny bit better?

- If you think politicians are on the make, register your protest by spoiling your ballot paper.

Shaking up the belief

Beliefs are anchored by two things: an initial experience, which creates the belief, and a series of confirming experiences. You can shake up the belief by offering some experiences which will not confirm the belief. Here are a couple of tactics:

- You say that politicians are pretty much the same; take a look at their election literature and tell me three things that are *different*. If you were to vote, which one would you choose?

- You say politicians are only in it for themselves; what things have politicians done that have benefited *other people*? If you were to vote, what would you look for?

Challenging the belief

The hardest approach is to challenge the underlying belief in order to influence the behaviour you want. For this, you will require compelling evidence and a persuasive approach. Here are a couple of tactics:

- Your children are at school, so I am sure their education is important to you. Candidate A says this about education in our area. Candidate B says something different. If you could influence things, which would you prefer?

- In the last four years, Candidate A has done this for the community here and Candidate B has done that. On that evidence, which candidate do you think would do more good if elected?

Values

The deepest level of our motivation is our values. These are the ultimate principles we live by and therefore the drivers of our decisions. Our values tell us what is important to us and are therefore very difficult to change. Most people do not consciously examine their values as adults; instead, they our values tell us what is important to us and are therefore very difficult to change

adopt values that are moulded by their upbringing and earlier experiences: their parents and carers, their schooling, their religion (or not), their friends, the people they observe and their community.

Matching values

If you understand another person's values, then you are able to ensure that your proposals and requests are consistent with them. This will remove a huge barrier from their willingness to say "yes". Typical examples include values around:

- *Fairness and equity.* Some people have a deep sense of what is just, and if something does not seem equitable to them, then their values will block them from supporting it.

- *Integrity and honesty.* We all like to think of ourselves in this way, but some will hold this value closer than others. You must find out what standards they hold to in assessing the meaning, to them, of integrity.

- *Politeness and manners.* Perhaps the way you ask seems immaterial to you, but, to some, courtesy is a vital part of how they socialise and do business. A good influencer will take great care to understand the cultural norms of the society you are influencing within, and how each individual interprets them.

- *Spheres of life.* Everybody has to juggle a complex set of relationships that form overlapping parts of their life: family, friends, social clubs, workplace, voluntary commitments and more. You need to understand the relative priorities and perceived obligations if you want to get your influencing process right.

- *Money and material goods.* This is the importance people attach to material wealth and how they value money and goods. For some, this is an important part of their lives that dominates their thinking; for others it is purely incidental – or even irrelevant.

Finally, don't dismiss the powerful role that religion and philosophy play in some people's lives. You may or may not have your own views, and they may or may not be strongly held. But some people do have religious, spiritual or related convictions that go beyond beliefs and so influence every decision they make. If you do not understand these values and how they can affect choices, you will fail to influence effectively.

Changing values

Given that values tend not to be based on objective decisions linked to external evidence, only I can change my values and influencing me to do so requires my permission. I am only likely to want to amend my values if I recognise that they are not serving me well and that the decisions I am making are poor ones. So, to influence a change in values, you need to show me how I make my decisions and help me understand the roles my values play in them.

Here are some examples of values that people may be prepared to re-evaluate, when confronted with evidence that the choices they generate are not giving them what they want in life.

- *"Risk is bad. I need to avoid it."* This value can lead to boredom, frustration and the inability to pursue goals driven by other values.

- *"I have to be perfect – nothing less will do."* This value will ultimately lead to disappointment. Early in our lives, perfection may be achievable – gold stars and ten-out-of-ten at school are possible. As we progress in our lives, we will exhaust ourselves pursuing an unattainable gold-standard.

- *"I have to please the people around me."* If you fear rejection too much, you will value other people's opinions of you above the value you place on yourself. Again this can hold you back from fulfilling your own dreams.

● "*I have to take responsibility for everything that goes wrong.*" This value leads to constant guilt. When you can show it stifles creativity or leads to destructive behaviours, people may be open to re-evaluate what they take responsibility for: themselves.

Find out by asking

The simplest way for you to find out what's in it for me is to ask. Of course there will be many times when the blunt question: "What do you want?" will not be appropriate. Instead, take an interest in me: ask questions about myself, my interests and what's important to me. These sort of questions will hook my "What's in it for me?" reflex.

brilliant example

You want me to sponsor your Sport Relief activity.

"Do you do a lot of sport?" you ask.

"No" I reply, uninterested.

"Do you raise much money for charity then?"

"Some", I say, not wanting to appear too mean.

"But when it comes to sport, you'd rather someone else did it for you?"

"Yup", thinking I can escape.

"What sort of charities would you support if you did raise some money?"

Now I am interested; I know exactly what causes are important to me.

"Did you know that Sport Relief is supporting two local charities that do just that?"

"No, I didn't, that's good."

"If you support my run, I'll make sure I finish so that you can support those charities."

"OK."

Questions to elicit decision criteria

Some of the questions that you can use to understand some-body's decision-making criteria are:

- What things are most important to you about ...?
- How will you decide whether to ...?
- What factors would you consider, when thinking about ...?
- How would you know if you had made the right decision about ...?
- What do you need to be most careful about, with ...?
- What would ... need to do/have to say to convince you it was right?
- When you did ... before, what were the most important things you learned?

Find out without asking

Asking is straightforward, but wouldn't it be great if you could figure out what I am thinking without asking?

 **impact**

Six ways to ask without asking:

1 Research my earlier decisions, actions or statements.

2 Talk to people who know me.

3   Get to know me better in general.

4   Ask me about other, similar circumstances.

5   Tell me about what others have done or are doing and gauge my reactions.

6   Figure out what you would do if you were me.

Figuring out what you would do if you were me

If you want to know how someone else is thinking, you have to put yourself in their position. This may sound tricky, but it is actually quite straightforward, and the following six-step process will take you through it. The better you know the other person, the more powerful the results will be.

> You never really understand a person until you consider things from his point of view – until you climb into his skin and walk around in it.

Spoken by Atticus Finch in *To Kill a Mockingbird* by Harper Lee

Step 1: Prepare a list of questions

Before you start to put yourself in someone else's position, consider carefully what questions you would like to ask them. Come up with a small number – two or three would be ideal – of vital things you would most like to know. These are the things you would ask them if you had the opportunity and knew you would get an honest answer. Write them in a list.

Step 2: Set up your physical space

Find yourself a quiet space where you will not be disturbed and take a position in that space where you feel comfortable. Take your list with you.

Close your eyes and imagine the other person coming into the space and making themselves comfortable. Use all of your experiences of them to imagine it as realistically as possible. Notice where they are and what posture they take: are they sitting or standing, upright or slouched? What expression do they have and what are they doing with their hands? Imagine you have asked them about this topic, and notice how they behave in response.

Step 3: Step into their place
Now, open your eyes, breathe deeply, and move to the position where you imagined the other person to be. Adopt the position and posture that you visualised and gently close your eyes.

Step 4: Climb into their skin
With your eyes closed, let your posture, your expression and your gestures become as much like those of the person you are imagining as you can. Get a feel of what it must be like to be them, considering this issue. Notice how your posture shifts, notice your breathing, notice how tense or relaxed you feel.

Now take some time to think about their concerns: what is important, what really matters, what do they want?

Step 5: Take a walk around
Now take a look at the list of questions. Read the first one and think about it, as that other person. Allow your eyes to close again. In their position, in their skin, how do you feel about it? Think about their concerns and their priorities; what answers come to mind? Notice the answers you get; how do you feel? How is your posture changing, and your breathing, and tensions in your body? What do you learn?

When you have nothing more to learn about the first question, have a look at the second and repeat the process.

Step 6: Return to your own skin

When you have completed the questions and learned all you can, open your eyes and take a few deep breaths. Now return to your original position, give your body a bit of a shake, and then relax back into being you. Take a few minutes to think about what you have learned from this process. What new insights do you have? How will this change the way you will try to influence the other person?

Altruism?

Do we always act purely in our own self-interest? Certainly not. As an influencer, it is wise to remember that. What we do often care about is the people we care about, so don't just ask "What's in it for you?", ask also, "What's in it for the people you care about?" Most of us will do more for the people we love and respect than we will do for ourselves.

 **brilliant** recap

- Self-interest is often an important motivator, so find ways to influence people to do or think what is to their advantage.

- The simplest way to find out "What's in it for me" is to ask me.

- If you cannot or do not want to ask me, then find out as much as you can about me, and then step into my skin.

- Always remember that we humans will sometimes put our self-interest behind that of others and, in particular, those we care most about.

CHAPTER 8

How to negotiate to share benefits

Why do so many businesses give away advice, in the form of booklets, newsletters and articles on the internet?

You already know that these give-aways are influential because, as well as carrying their sponsor's brand (familiarity breeds like-ableness), they establish the company's credibility too. But there is another powerful influencing technique they are using: the "I've-scratched-your-back-now-you-scratch-mine" principle. It works for chimpanzees and it works for people too.

This chapter is about the give and take of sharing benefits. In the first section, reciprocation, you will see why this give and take is so powerful and how to use it to build your influence. In the second section, negotiation, you will get a brief introduction to the process of negotiating, which is really just a search for a give and take that satisfies everyone.

Reciprocation

A sense of fairness drives many people. As an influencer, you have to remember that it will be hard to get anybody to agree to something that they do not see as fair.

⌁)brilliant insight

Equity theory

John Stacey Adams suggested that people need to feel they are getting what is fair from a relationship. If they believe that they are getting too little, they will feel resentment, anger or humiliation. If they believe that they are getting too much, they will feel greedy, guilty or ashamed. In either case, they will try to remove the unpleasant feelings by restoring balance. Adams referred to this as "equity theory".

A sense of fairness can help you to influence others. Our sense of equity means that if you offer something freely, then people will recognise that, and be keen to return the favour.

> a sense of fairness can help you to influence others.

Give and take

Give and take can operate at three levels and, whilst all levels work equally well, they are increasingly subtle, and therefore increasingly powerful as tools of influence.

Gifts

Have you ever been to a Christmas party or something similar where you and your friends routinely exchange gifts? When it comes to the time for exchange, you open the first gift from one friend and realise that they have spent considerably more money than you did. Your gift to them is a token, yet you find that they have clearly given you something of substance. How do you feel?

Most people will find this very uncomfortable and would wish they had spent more. There are some people who record the gifts that they are given by friends, to ensure that the gifts they return are proportionate and ensure the balance is maintained.

The giving and receiving of gifts is long established as a part of the social and commercial "glue" of most – maybe all – cultures. Problems arise when we enter an unfamiliar culture in which gifts are interpreted differently: my gift is your baksheesh, or their bribe.

What makes gifts particularly powerful is that it is hard to say "no". Indeed, in saying "no", we do not negate the power of the gift to trigger reciprocity and, arguably, we enhance it: now, not only have you offered me a gift, but I have rejected it.

Examples of the use of gifts include small tokens given by charities or their collectors, introductory offers, and informative reports available on the internet. The last of these is also a good example of how gifts can be devalued by being too readily available. Some websites and marketing schemes offer so many free gifts that people come to realise that they can accumulate them without obligation. Those people can then start to resent the suggestion that they may be charged for a product or service in the future.

Use gifts with great care: make sure that they are acceptable within the culture you are operating in and cannot cause offence or embarrassment. Finally, give gifts that are proportionate to the relationship. If the gift is too big, it will trigger alarm bells, rather than a sense of reasonable obligation.

Favours

More subtle than gifts are favours. When you do me a favour, I feel in your debt and we often hear the phrase "I owe you one". People recognise a favour as having real value because it involves your time, rather than just a financial element, which gifts represent. Influential people make a habit of doing favours for all sorts of people in all sorts of contexts.

We might be talking one day. I suggest that I am interested in how to give feedback to one of my work colleagues. If you have recently read an article on the subject, you might mention it and then say, "I'll tell you what – I still have that article, so I will copy it and pop the copy in the post". This is an easy favour to grant, but one that has real value to me.

You can take it a step further. Three weeks ago, when we met, we were talking about how to get bigger crops from my vegetable patch. Today you spot an article on that subject in the colour supplement of your weekend newspaper. So you cut it out, put it in an envelope and post it to me with a short, handwritten note, saying you remember our conversation and thought I might be interested in this article.

If you do that, you have done me two favours:

- You have taken an interest in what I am interested in – and remembered it.

- You have taken the trouble to send me something relevant.

As a "gift" this has no material value so there will be no embarrassment in my receiving it. As a favour, however, it has huge value, because it is directly relevant to my needs or desires.

 **tip**

The power of secrets

One of the biggest favours I can do you is to grant you access to a secret. The sharing of secrets does more than create a sense of rapport through intimacy; it also creates a reciprocal obligation. A secret is like a gift.

Concessions

If I give up something I want, in response to your desires or needs, I am making a concession. As this helps you get what you want, you are likely to feel a sense of obligation to return the concession. Concessions work in two ways:

1 You make a request of me. It doesn't suit me to say "yes" and you know it, but I do say "yes".

2 I make a request of you. It doesn't suit you to say "yes", so I reduce or even remove my request.

Giving concessions will be an important part of negotiating and is one of the reasons why negotiators should always start by asking "big". This will give you the chance to offer a concession and say: "If you can't accept this, how about something less?"

▶ brilliant example

A well ordered jumble sale will start with the biggest and highest-priced objects near the entrance. Then the tables will contain successively lower-value items. As you leave, there will be a stall selling raffle tickets. "Not bought anything today? Well I am sure you'd like some raffle tickets."

The ideal follow-up would be something like "You can get 12 for £10".

If that's still too much: "That's all right, you can buy them for only £1 each – shall I put you down for five?"

A reciprocation economy

The determined influencer will look for opportunities to build a web of reciprocations that create an economy of traded favours, concessions and gifts. There are five steps to follow in a concerted programme of building your exchange network (see Figure 8.1).

Step 1: Build your network

Everyone you meet is a potential trading partner. The biggest mistake that inexperienced influencers make is to focus on the people whom they think can help them. How far can

> everyone you meet is a potential trading partner.

you see into the future? We don't know who can help us in a year's time – or ten – so instead, assume everyone can.

 **example**

There was a professor being interviewed on a television documentary, who talked with real insight into the way a number of the very top politicians are thinking. How did he come to know senior frontbenchers from all parties so well? The answer is that he couldn't. But he could get to know lots of junior politicians at the starts of their careers. And by staying in touch, and trading small favours, as they rose, so did the power of his connections.

Instead of building a network of people who can help you, focus on the people whom you can help.

Step 2: Understand your contacts
Get to know everyone: what interests them, concerns them, drives them. What are their needs, aspirations and desires? The more you know about people, the more chances you will have to do something for them.

Step 3: Offer trades
Now use your knowledge to do favours, proffer small gifts, and put people in touch with other people who can help them. You might think of each small gift or favour as a deposit in your "bank of influence".

Step 4: Harvest your investments
When you have made enough investments, you will start to reap the rewards in terms of favours returned, gifts given and concessions made. You will be able to access people's resources, knowledge and expertise. Perhaps more important will be their

connections and influence, which they may be prepared to lend to you, to help you get your projects going.

Step 5: Use their links

The final step, which will complete the cycle and return you to step 1, is to look after the network you have built, and use the contacts it gives you, to identify new connections that will help you to grow your network and build new reciprocity relationships. We will return to this topic in more detail in the next chapter.

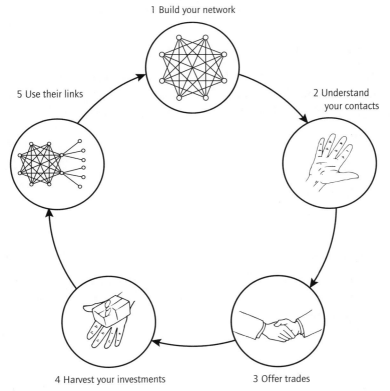

Figure 8.1 The five steps in building an exchange network

 **brilliant** tip

The internet offers many tools to help you manage your networks and create opportunities to offer help and respond to requests. There are:

● sites designed for social contacts like MySpace, Bebo and Facebook;

● sites designed to facilitate opinion sharing, like Wordpress, Windows Live Spaces and Twitter;

● sites designed to manage professional networks, like LinkedIn, Ecademy and Plaxo.

Negotiation

Negotiation is a process of searching for an agreement that satisfies all parties. It is a process, so it can be broken into distinct stages, and we will work with a simple four-stage model:

1 Preparation.

2 Opening.

3 Bargaining.

4 Closing.

Preparation

In many negotiations, the outcome is decided at the preparation stage. There is a lot to do here, so rushing your preparation is a false economy.

 **brilliant** impact

Failing to prepare = Preparing to fail.

Top and tail

Always begin preparing for your negotiation with a clear articulation of what you want to achieve and what you are prepared to settle for: your top and your tail. What you want to achieve is your goal, or your purpose in entering the negotiation. This is the outcome which you consider to be optimal for you. Your tail is the last outcome you would be prepared to accept. If the outcome were any worse than your tail, you would be better off not concluding an agreement. Therefore, to find your tail, you must look to see what alternatives you have to reaching an agreement. The value of your tail will match the value of the best of these alternatives.

Your top and tail represent the "what". You also need to give some thought to what you will be prepared to offer in return, and to the conditions you can expect to be applied.

Overlaps

A negotiation is like two overlapping circles. One circle represents all the things you want and the other represents the things the other person wants. If there is an overlap, then it is possible to reach agreement. In your preparation, think through everything you know about the contents of these circles:

- What do you need?   What do they need?
- What do you want?   What do they want?
- What are your priorities?   What are their priorities?
- What have you got to offer? What have they got to offer?

The more of these "negotiating variables" you can identify, the more flexibility you will have to reach a desirable agreement. For each variable, you also need to understand its value to you and to them. A great negotiating strategy will always be built on "differential values".

When something is worth more to them than it is to you, offering it makes an attractive offer to both sides. A common example is the extras car dealers offer towards the end of a negotiation to buy a car. If they offer to throw in a full set of floor mats, the dealer knows they will cost you between £50 and £100. The dealer, however, will probably only pay between £10 and £50 and will also be able to deduct the cost against their tax.

Details

The last stage of your preparation is to master the details. Have you or any of your friends or colleagues negotiated with this person before? If so, what can you learn from the experience? What information do you need to have ready to hand during the negotiation? Make sure you are familiar with the facts and can access the information quickly when you need it. Put together a plan for how you want to conduct the negotiation, including where you want to hold it. Finally, in your mind's eye, visualise a successful negotiation with a fair and desirable outcome.

Opening

The opening creates a joint basis for your negotiation and also creates an impression on both of you. There are three components to get right.

Influencing

Three of our rules of influencing come to the fore at the opening stage of your negotiations:

1   *Make a great first impression.* Dress for the negotiation and enter the shop, market place or room confidently. Make sure you are organised and ready.

2   *Take some time to build a rapport.* Negotiations are between people, so a few pleasantries will help activate the fairness drivers in both of you and make it easier to handle the tough stuff. In many cultures, this is a vital part of the negotiation process: as an example, I once over an hour

enjoying tea and chatting with a shopkeeper in Nepal before even starting the bargaining stage of negotiating for a carpet.

3   *Authority is critical in negotiating.* Always check what authority the person you are dealing with has. Are they able to make a binding commitment? If you are in any doubt that they are, you must never end your dealings with them by making your best offer. They will almost certainly go back to the final authority, who will demand extra concessions of you.

Rules

Now establish any ground rules for the negotiation: for example, who will be involved and any time constraints.

Kick-off

We often kick off the bargaining stage of a negotiation with each party stating what they hope to achieve: their objectives. Normally, each side will try to manoeuvre the other into stating their objectives first. This is because if my objective is to pay less than £100 and yours is to settle for a price of £80 or over, if I go first, you will rapidly change your objective.

The only time to state your objective first is when you want to change perceptions around the whole negotiation. Since the first speaker will usually set the frame for the negotiation, if your requirements are radical, then get them articulated first. It must then be the other person who objects. When you make your first concession, you will take control of the reciprocity trading. If the other person were to speak first, it will be you who is objecting and they will have the advantage.

Bargaining

The bargaining stage is often mistaken for the whole negotiation. This is where all your preparation will pay off.

There are five bargaining strategies. These are based on different balance points between two things: achieving your goal, and protecting and strengthening your relationship with the person you are negotiating with.

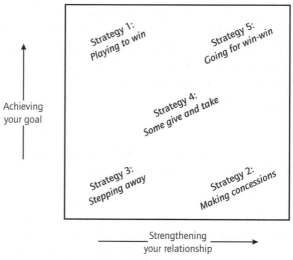

Figure 8.2 The five bargaining strategies

Strategy 1: Playing to win

When you go into a shop in a foreign country, and you know you will never return, your relationship with the shopkeeper is of little or no consequence to you. You want the best possible deal and will not mind greatly if you come across as a lovely person or as mean spirited. The shopkeeper may well try to draw you into rapport but do not mistake this for a genuine desire to build a relationship. They probably want you to start to care how they may perceive you and soften your approach.

Play to win when there are no consequences to damaging the relationship or when winning is of overriding importance to you.

Strategy 2: Making concessions

The opposite end of the spectrum is where your desire to maintain and enhance the relationship far exceeds the importance of the outcome. You will be prepared to sacrifice your goal, or significant chunks of it, to prevent a weakening of the relationship, or to enhance it. Shops that offer "loss leader" goods that are priced below their value are doing so to build a relationship with new customers, to draw them in and, they hope, trigger reciprocity to encourage further spending. Be careful with this strategy – be sure the relationship is important to you and also that concessions will really enhance it.

Strategy 3: Stepping away

There are times when negotiating can bring no good. There may be no overlap between the circles representing what you and the other person want, or the timing may be wrong. It may be that the value of the outcome is so low as not to justify negotiating. In any of these cases, step away entirely, or take a break until the time is right to resume the negotiation.

This strategy prioritises neither the relationship nor your goal and works when neither is of great importance to you.

Strategy 4: Some give and take

Good old compromise involves each party being prepared to make concessions to the other until both are satisfied that the outcome is equitable. In the process, both parties will achieve less than their top goal and, in conceding, will feel just a little bit taken advantage of. Whilst the give-and-take strategy balances goal and relationship, neither one is optimised.

Strategy 5: Going for win-win

"Win-win" negotiating takes most effort and returns greatest benefit. If, instead of examining what they are prepared to concede, each party also looks at what they are prepared to add into the negotiation, they can build a solution that meets and exceeds each of their goals and, in so doing, builds their relationship through genuine collaboration and the mutual respect it engenders.

The "win-win" strategy is time consuming and hard work, so is justified only when the potential end result is worth the effort. If you ever hear someone suggest that all negotiations should be "win-win", question their perspective.

Offers

During the bargaining phase, each party will make and receive many offers. There are only three options for any offer you receive.

1 *It may be spot on.* In this case confirm it, accept it, and move to close.

2 *It may not sound very good to you.* In this case, remember that it is only an offer. Understand it, assess it, and make a counter-offer.

3 *It may sound too good to be true.* In this case, proceed with extreme caution and take your time in examining it very carefully.

 If it sounds too good to be true; it usually is.

Concessions

Here are three great rules to follow when called upon to make a concession.

1 *When asked for a concession, always make your first response a defence.* If you give in too easily, you will devalue the concession and they will want another straight away.

2 *Only make a concession if you get something in return.* Make a list of everything you can ask for. Before you commit to your concession, say something like "I could make a concession, but let's see what you can do in return". This is

a great opportunity to look for something of high value to you, but low value to them. The act of asking for something in return signals that your concession has real value.

3 *If you must make concessions, make them small and of decreasing value.* What do you need to concede to get agreement? Then halve it! You are likely to be called upon to make more concessions, so if your first is too big then the cumulative value may take you below your tail. If each concession is half the value of the previous one, the cumulative value will be limited to twice the value of the first concession you make.

Closing

One of the biggest mistakes of inexperienced negotiators is to reach a good agreement in the bargaining stage and then to leave it hanging, without sealing the deal. The process of sealing the deal is called "closing".

Seal the deal ...

If you recall the end of Chapter 3, we looked at a number of ways to close a decision. These apply equally to negotiations.

 **impact**

Six negotiation closers

1 The direct ask:
   "I think we have reached a fair agreement. Do you agree?"
   "Shall we shake hands on this agreement?"

2 The summary and ask:
   "So, we have agreed this and this. Are you ready to conclude an agreement now?"

3 The conditional ask:
   "If I were to offer this one last concession, could you then agree to ...?"

4 The one more ask:
  "If you were to offer this one last concession, I would be ready to agree it straight away."

5 The presumptive ask:
  "So, would you like a coffee while we sign the paperwork?"

6 The either-or ask:
  "Would you like the free delivery, or the 60-day payment terms?"

... and keep it sealed

Salespeople have a wonderful term: the "buy back". Let's suppose you have spent nearly an hour in the mobile phone shop carefully selecting a new phone. You are very happy with your choice and the salesperson is just sorting through the papers so they can make out your contract. As they do so, they make a throwaway remark:

"What a great choice you've made. It's a fabulous new model and you are the first person who has bought one of these."

"A new model?" you ask. You did not know that.

"Yes," says the salesperson, "they only came in this morning and have only been on the market since Monday – you are very lucky."

If you are one of those people who loves "new" you will doubtless feel even better about your purchase. But what if you are now worried about the reliability of a new model that may not have been tested properly and wanted something totally reliable. Never mind the manufacturer's reputation, now you have doubts.

"I see. Can you give me some time to think about this?" you say, putting your credit card away and preparing to leave the shop. The salesperson has lost the sale and "bought back" the deal.

Once you have closed the deal, there is nothing you can say that can make it any better, so anything you do say can only be pointless at best or destructive at worst. When you have closed a deal, confine all your comments to process and pleasantries.

 brilliant recap

- Our sense of fairness is fundamental, so we are compelled to reciprocate any gifts, favours or concessions.

- Build an economy of "give and take" among your friends, colleagues and contacts to create a network of influence.

- Negotiation may seem daunting, but it follows a simple four-step process of preparation, opening, bargaining and closing.

- Once you have closed your deal, shut up.

CHAPTER 9

How to network to help people help you

B y now, you should be feeling confident that you can influence the people around you. Building up your influence further means making opportunities to give, and in Chapter 8 you saw a five-step process for creating and strengthening your "reciprocation economy". This chapter is about having more people whom you can influence. It will focus on steps 1 (how you can build your network) and 5 (how you can maintain and extend your network). In doing so, we will introduce five key attributes you need to cultivate in yourself – patience, courage, curiosity, enthusiasm and commitment.

How to build a network

The essential personal attribute for building a network is patience. We need to build our networks one person at a time. Any attempt to do otherwise will leave you with weak connections that will be of no use to you. You will have no influence over people with whom you do not have a personal connection so, unless you think of networking as a form of stamp-collecting where numbers have a value, this approach will waste your time.

> the essential personal attribute for building a network is patience

Be wary of people who claim many hundreds of contacts. Unless networking is fundamentally their business and they are making real time for those people, they will be merely names on a list.

Where to build a network

You can build your network anywhere: everyone is interesting and everyone may one day be a useful contact. There are, however, some excellent places to start.

brilliant tip

Everyone is interesting, so make a point of getting to know younger people, more junior people and people at the starts of their careers. Just because they don't have seniority or experience, it is unwise to think of them as being uninteresting or of little value to you. You have no way of knowing how their future and their career may progress. If you take an active interest in people at the start of their career, or at a low point, then as they rise, so does the value of their friendship. Remember that networking is like investing.

Here are four places where you can build your network.

At work

The best way to extend your network is to volunteer for discretionary activities that will give you a chance to meet and work with new people. If that is not an option, then make good use of times when you can meet people you don't normally speak with – at the starts and ends of breaks, at starts and ends of the day, and when you get refreshments.

At play

Social groups and sports clubs are great opportunities to build a network of people with different backgrounds and jobs to yours. If you are in a sports club that competes against other clubs, look for the chance to meet some of your competitors – this will open your net even wider. Voluntary activities like fundraising, caring or environmental groups usually attract a particularly diverse range of participants. Some of them will seem to have little in common with you, so they may well add something new to your network. That quiet old gent who says little could once have worked with just the people you would love to speak with. If you don't start a conversation with him, you'll never know that; nor that he meets them all once a month.

On the margins
There are a range of activities that feel a bit like work and a bit like play. Whether it is training, trade association meetings, exhibitions, conferences or meetings of professional bodies, these activities are often designed to facilitate networking. Do not waste these opportunities.

On the web
In Chapter 8 there is a set of examples of websites that can help you with your networking. Online networking takes time and care. Approach this as any other networking opportunity: with patience. Choose which services to use, learn about them and start slowly, building up your skill and expertise. Remember that your objective should not be to build a big number of contacts but to enhance existing networks and use them to create some more high-quality links.

How to build a network
Meeting people and talking with them is only the start of building your network. There are two further things to do: you must remember them and you must make yourself memorable to them.

Remember them
Not only is it important to remember names; you must also

remember details. Lots of software companies offer clever solutions to recording the facts about your contacts and, of course, there is always a good old notebook. Spend time trying out a few different systems before deciding which one is for you. Once you have chosen, use it well. It is better to choose something simpler and adapt it to your needs than to go for a complex system that you will find a chore to use and will therefore not make good use of.

Make yourself memorable

Once you have made contact, look for opportunities to refresh that contact. Offer help or do small favours, like sending links to interesting and relevant web resources. A few calls or emails early on will cement your relationship and help you to establish whether it will be a close one early on, or part of your wider network.

How to make use of networking opportunities

Networking is one of those activities that feature frequently in people's list of least favourite things to do. The idea of walking into a room full of strangers and starting a conversation with one of them fills many of us with dread. Here is the key: they are strangers. So if the worst happens and you don't strike a rapport, then you need never see them again. So what is there to lose?

However, to really go for it, there are three key attributes for this, the hardest part of networking: courage, curiosity and enthusiasm.

Courage

It really does take courage to start a conversation with a stranger, so have pity on all those people in the room who are scared to approach you. Be kind to them. Make it easy for them by going to them. Now be the one to break the ice and say "hello". There is a simple four-step process which sounds insultingly obvious. At the risk of insulting you:

1 Gap. Wait for a gap when people are not talking – or, better still, approach someone who is on their own.

2 Smile. It helps to look like you are pleased to meet them and a smile will break the ice. You will look more confident and likeable and will put the other person at their ease.

3 Greet. Rapport building starts with a friendly greeting. The exchange of a formality will put both of you at your ease because we all know the format.

4 Name. Once you have exchanged greetings, introduce yourself. Offer your name and your hand. The secret to a good handshake is to adapt it to the other person: firm, but not too firm, with your hand approaching theirs, aligned vertically with your thumb up.

brilliant tip

Have a badge made up. Get yourself a smart name badge with your name in clear and easy-to-read type. This will make you more memorable and take away other people's fear of forgetting your name – and therefore make you more appealing to speak to than what's-their-name-in-blue-over-there.

Curiosity

The best tip for how to network well in a room full of new people is to be curious. Ask yourself: "What can I learn from each of these people?" If you assume that each person in that room has some interesting information for you, whether it's a great story, a fascinating fact, or a shared passion, you will not only make better company and a better companion, you will learn more too.

There are three things to do with each person you meet: ask them questions, listen attentively to their answers, and take an interest in what they are saying. If you let me talk about me, two things happen: first, you learn a lot more than if you talk about yourself; and, second, I will think you an excellent conversationalist. After all, you are talking about my favourite subject; we all like to talk about ourselves.

Listen in particular for opportunities to offer me help or to put me in touch with someone.

Enthusiasm

Once you get talking with me, it can be tempting to stay talking with me. The hardest part is breaking the ice. The value of a networking opportunity is in meeting a range of people, so after around ten minutes, it is time to move on. If there is more for us to talk about, then we can meet up again, and further strengthen our link. A good way to politely move on is to introduce me to somebody else in the room, whom you have met. Once I get talking with them, you can move on. If I find them to be interesting, then I will mentally log the favour you have done me and you will have made your first deposit in our shared reciprocation economy.

brilliant tip

At various points in the event, create a moment to consolidate your memory of what you have learned about me. For most people, that means making notes. Use your notebook, or the back of the business card I have given you.

Maintain and extend your network

For maintaining and extending your network, the key attitude is commitment.

Stay in touch

Make time to stay in touch with each person in your network. For many, this need only be once every three to six months. The less close they are, the more likely you are to lose your ability to influence them if you stay out of contact for too long. Use the phone, cards or emails, or, if you have invested the time in connecting with them through one or more web-based services, these can help enormously.

From time to time, look for an opportunity to meet up. If you are visiting their area and can free up half an hour for a drink or a coffee, then drop them a line and suggest it. Even if they cannot make it, the invitation shows you are willing to stay in touch and interested enough in them to offer some of your time to see them.

Introduce people

Don't just wait to be asked for a contact. When you meet someone new who may have an overlapping interest with someone you already know, drop them both a line suggesting they may have something in common. Then leave it with them either to pursue it or not. The quality and relevance of the connections that you offer people will dictate the value they attach to them, so this stage will grow slowly as your network grows.

And so we come full circle: you need patience.

 **brilliant** recap

- Build your network one person at a time, taking every opportunity to speak to new people and add them to your contact list.

- At events where you have the chance to meet lots of new people, summon up your courage and introduce yourself. Take an interest in them and you will learn lots about them and make them feel at ease.

● Stay committed to each person in your network and look for ways to stay in touch, contacting each person at least once a year.

CHAPTER 10

The six top influencing techniques

When you want to achieve anything in life, the best way to do it is to find a process that works and follow it. This is not intended to exempt you from critical thinking – if the process is wrong, then it won't work. And remember that a process that is right for one situation may not be right for another, which may look superficially similar.

All the ideas in this book are based on experience and research. If your proposition is a good one and you present it well, you will be able to convince me. If you build up enough credit with me by making yourself likeable, credible and respected, I will listen to you. If you apply the right pressure by using your understanding of my psychology in an ethical way, it will be to you that I offer my help, support and loyalty.

Let us put together what you have learned to create processes for achieving influence in six common situations:

Winning an argument

1 *Be clear about your outcome*
Know what you are trying to achieve and its purpose. Be sure to distinguish this from the details which might be negotiable.

2 *Start with small talk*
Allow a little time for small talk to establish rapport.
People are far more likely to give concessions to someone with whom they have a personal contact.

3 *We disagree, so let me speak first*
This will give you a better idea of my argument and also leave me feeling I then need to listen to you (the "I've-scratched-your-back-now-you-scratch-mine" principle).

4 *Slice up the pie*
Look for points of agreement to minimise the area of conflict and build on the rapport you have.

5 *Remain flexible*
If you know what your outcome is, be as adaptable as possible in the way you achieve it. Listen for opportunities to agree, which can move the argument in the right direction.

6 *Keep off the trivia*
Separate essential details from trivia and ensure that you don't let the trivia devalue your credibility.

7 *Listen with 100% of your attention*
While the other person is speaking, listen to them. There will be time to think through your response when they have finished: if you do it while they are speaking, you may miss an important point.

8 *Establish your credibility*
Use robust evidence and plain language to support your argument. Where possible, present independent and authoritative facts to back you up and ensure that the logical flow of your conclusions is flawless.

9 *Find supporters*
The more authoritative and credible they are, the better. The more of them there are, the better. Best of all are people that can endorse your point of view that will be seen by the person you are arguing with as "like me".

10 *Give them an escape route*   .
No one likes to change their mind. So give some tiny new fact or argument that "you may not have considered" which gives the other person a chance to agree with you without backing down.

Influencing me to do you a favour or help you out

1 *Build up credit with me*
Long before you ever need a favour from me, make sure I like you and respect you so that I will want to help you. Put yourself out for me and do me small favours, so that when you come to need help, I already feel that I am in your debt.

2 *Ask for a much smaller favour in advance*
If you ask a small favour of me, I can easily oblige. Having once granted you a favour, it would be inconsistent of me to turn you down in the future, so I am far more likely to say "yes".

3 *Give me notice so I can schedule it*
If I like to control my time, a sudden change of plan will be unwelcome. Give me advance warning and I can plan it in. This has the added effect that a task seems smaller while it is a long way off. As it approaches, it may seem bigger, but if I have already made a commitment, then I will want to keep my word.

4 *Pick your moment*
Avoid asking me for a favour when I am busy, rushed or focused on something else.

5 *Be very precise in what you ask for*
If you ask me for 70 minutes of my time, I will be a lot more confident you know exactly what is involved than if you ask me for an hour.

6   *Give me a reason*
Use the power of "because" to give me a reason to put
myself out for you. Whatever reasons you give, do not
leave me thinking you are in a fix because of your own
foolishness. If you are, then at least show me you have
the wisdom to avoid making the same mistake in the
future.

7   *Make it self-contained*
A simple task is easier to do and the gratification of
completing it will seem easy to achieve. If the task seems
open-ended or ambiguous, I will feel as if you are asking
me to sign a blank cheque with my calendar.

8   *Portray it as a continuation of something I'm already doing*
Starting something new is hard: continuing something I
have already started feels a lot easier.

9   *Show me that you are also helping yourself*
I may want to help you, but I am no mug: I don't want to
do everything for you. Let me know that you are working
hard on your own behalf too.

10 *Let me know you are relying on me*
If I think that there are other people you can ask, then I
have an easy get-out. If I know that there is no one else
who can help you, then I am far more likely to step in.

11 *Presuppose that I will say "yes"*
While it is very dangerous to give me no choice (which
will trigger reactance – the "black is white" effect), act
as if you expect me to say "yes". If you are confident I
will say "yes", I will feel a pressure to conform with your
expectations.

12 *Tell me what's in it for me*
What do I stand to gain from helping you out? Appeal to
my self-interest by showing me how I can benefit.

And finally:

13 *If at first you don't succeed – keep trying*
Don't assume I won't help you: I may just not be able
or willing to help you *now*. Salespeople know that it
sometimes takes six or seven sales calls to make the sale.
Persistence often pays off when all else fails.

Influencing me to get going with something

1 *Don't give me too much choice*
If I have too many choices I may well get stuck just trying
to decide.

2 *Give me clear step-by-step instructions*
This makes each step seem easy, so I can dive in without
fear.

3 *Give me a specific number of steps*
If I feel the task is endless, I will be daunted. A specific
number of steps makes the task finite. The smaller that
number is, the better; and George Miller's magic number
suggests seven steps should be the maximum for a task I
do not fancy.

4 *Make the first step particularly small and simple*
This will create the minimum barrier to getting started and
I will gain some momentum.

5 *Let me know others have already made a start*
Trigger my need to feel on the inside of the group, rather
than isolated.

6 *Be clear what you expect of me*
This way, I know what to do to meet your expectations.

7 *Create success points*
Let me see a finishing line – even right at the start – by
creating milestones where I can see and celebrate progress.

8 *Create time pressure*
Many of us work best with a deadline.

9 *Choose your time*
It feels easier to start something at "landmark" times like the start of the day, after a break, or on the hour. Landmark days are also important: for example, Mondays or the first of the month.

10 *Start something yourself at the same time*
Roll up your sleeves and either work with me or let me see you getting started on something too. Work is always easier in company.

Influencing me to keep my promise

1 *Ask me to make a promise*
The first step is to secure a promise from me. Ask me to make a commitment and wait until I do. Better still, ask for it in front of other people.

2 *Ask me to commit to a deadline*
Promises attached to a specific timeframe are even more powerful.

3 *Let me know that you know I made a promise*
Acknowledge my promise and thank me for it, so that I know you are aware of it.

4 *Find out how I plan to keep it*
If you enquire gently into my plans, I will have to start to engage my mind in the process of fulfilling my commitment to you, adding further layers of commitment.

5 *Attach consequences to my promise*
Let me know how my promise is important and what the consequences will be if I do not keep it.

6 *Test the strength of my commitment*
If you ask me "What would keep you from fulfilling your commitment?" you will soon establish its strength. If I give a robust reason, particularly one that is out of my control, I am thinking in terms of keeping my promise. If I respond with a wishy-washy "You know, things can go wrong" sort of statement, then you can be sure I will be looking out for a chance to renege on my promise.

7 *Lay out expectations*
Let me know that you are confident that I will keep my word. Better still, let me know who else is expecting me to do what I said I would.

8 *Remind me of promises you have kept*
Do this subtly, but do trigger my need to repay you for favours you have done for me, which meant you had to keep your word when you may not have wanted to.

Influencing me to change my mind

1 *Show me unforeseen consequences*
Are there any consequences of my position that could be damaging? Let me see them and tell me how I can mitigate them by adopting a different position.

2 *Avoid blame*
Show that you understand my position and that you can see why it is an entirely reasonable one to have taken.

3 *Take me for a walk*
You may find that my position is, in my unconscious mind, tied to my physical position. Taking me to a new place will literally allow me to see things from a different point of view. Getting me moving will literally help get my thinking moving.

4 *Give me the credit for your point of view*
Show me how your perspective is consistent with
something I have said or done in the past and that it is
entirely consistent with who I am.

5 *Show me how my position is inconsistent*
This is more dangerous. You may be able to demonstrate
an inconsistency in my point of view, which will at least
lead me to challenge it for myself.

6 *Ask me how critics would perceive my position*
If you can encourage me to see my ideas from another
perspective, I may spot the flaw that you have spotted.

7 *Stay committed*
Your commitment to your point of view, and your
enthusiasm for it, may influence me to at least reassess my
thinking.

8 *Show me other people who oppose my interpretation*
The more people whom I consider well-informed and with
similar perspectives to my own, but who do not share my
opinion, the more pressure I will feel to re-examine it for
myself.

9 *Introduce new information*
Give me a reason to change my mind that allows me
to save face and not back down. In the context of new
information, I am not "changing my mind", I am "acting
on new information".

10 *Make concessions yourself*
If you want me to concede something, then trigger my
desire to reciprocate by making your own concession.

Influencing me to forgive you

 When you're wrong, 'fess-up, say you're sorry and move on.

Folk wisdom

1 *Admit you are wrong*
Own up to your mistake.

2 *Take responsibility*
If the mistake was truly due to circumstances outside your control, there is nothing to forgive. Otherwise, accept your responsibility for the mistake you made, without excuse.

3 *Say you are sorry*
Make an unconditional apology, including the words "I am sorry". Look me in the eyes when you say them.

4 *Accept the consequences*
Recognise that there are consequences to your error and readily accept those that will fall upon you. This may include a punishment. If a punishment is appropriate, then be the first to mention it and suggest a harsh one. That way, I will be the one pressuring for leniency.

5 *Show regret*
Let me know that you regret what has happened, and what you propose to do that will move in the direction of putting things right. Do not pretend that you can make everything all right again if you know that you cannot.

6 *Look forward*
Tell me what you will do differently in the future to ensure you do not make the same mistake again. Demonstrate that you have understood what happened and why it happened, that you have learned from the event, and that you have made changes that will prevent a similar recurrence.

7   *Make a commitment*

Once I have accepted your analysis of what went wrong and how to avoid it happening again, look me in the eyes again and commit to doing what you say you will do.

8   *Move on*

You do not need to keep referring back to the incident, but neither must you forget it. The best way to show me that you haven't forgotten is to constantly keep delivering on your commitment.

 **brilliant** recap

● Following a process will give you the best chance of success in influencing the people around you.

● This means:

   1 be clear about what exactly you want to achieve;

   2 put together some of these techniques and try them out;

   3 notice what happens;

   4 figure out what worked and what didn't work and, if you need to, alter your approach.

● Be persistent and remain focused, adaptable and resilient to get the results you want.

● Evaluate each situation and apply a combination of the techniques you know.

Conclusion

The techniques in this book all work but, to become a truly brilliant influencer, you'll need to combine elements from each chapter, depending on your situation. Try putting techniques together, try the combinations out, notice what happens, and then figure out what worked and what didn't work and, if you need to, alter your approach.

Remember, too, that your attitude is key – you need to be:

- *Persistent.* If something is important, keep working at it until you get what you want.
- *Flexible.* If something is not working, persist. But adapt yourself, by trying different approaches.
- *Resilient.* If you are not getting what you want, stay focused, remain confident, and recognise that other people do have the right to say "no".

It is no coincidence that these are three of the attitudes that we identified in Chapter 1 as attitudes that contribute to your influence. This is not just because they are central to your success but because these are attractive attitudes which most of us like, respect and value in the people we encounter.

Ultimately, influence is a human activity of either intentional or unintentional communication. We cannot help but influence each other; what we can do is practise behaviours, language and techniques that have the effects we want. If some work in one situation, and not in another, then let us celebrate the diversity of humankind.

With integrity, conviction and the tools you have learned, you are ready.

What did you think of this book?

We're really keen to hear from you about this book, so that we can make our publishing even better.

Please log on to the following website and leave us your feedback.

It will only take a few minutes and your thoughts are invaluable to us.

www.pearsoned.co.uk/bookfeedback

Glossary

Altruism   We don't always do things just for our own benefit; we sometimes act purely for other people.

Because   We are influenced when we can understand the reason for a request. "Because ..." gives us a reason.

"Black and white" effect   We evaluate a thing in the context of the other things around it.

"Black is white" effect   We sometimes react against what others try to impose on us. Also called "reactance".

BLUF   Bottom Line Up Front.

"Doing what's expected" effect   We tend to conform to the expectations of the people around us.

"Eight-out-of-ten-cat-owners" principle   We are influenced by what other people, like us, do.

Framing   Setting the context for what follows.

"I'm-gorgeous-fly-me" principle   We are influenced by people whom we like.

"I've-scratched-your-back-now-you-scratch-mine" principle   We are influenced by a favour or a concession to reciprocate, and offer a favour or concession in return.

"Jiminy Cricket" effect   Formally known as "cognitive dissonance", the discomfort we feel when we are about to do something that contradicts our own moral code.

Journalists' principle Less is more – eliminate extra words that do not add to your argument.

"Let-me-introduce-you-to-my-friend" principle We are influenced by testimonials and references from other people.

Mark Antony's principle People remember your mistakes more readily than they recall everything you get right.

Matching Consciously being like someone else in one way or another.

Mirroring Copying somebody's body posture so that your posture looks to them as their own would if viewed in a mirror.

"Narrower is deeper" effect We find a narrow expertise more credible than a general competence.

Negotiation A process of searching for an agreement that satisfies all parties.

Network The people you have contact with, whom you can influence and who can also influence others on your behalf.

"One-chance-to-make-a-first-impression" principle The first impression you make on somebody will frame their interpretation of everything you say or do.

Personal power Your credibility, personality, character and integrity which makes you influential.

Power words Some words have a strong, positive impact on a listener or reader.

PPaP Position, Pressure, ask, Point of view.

Presence The way someone can draw other people's attention towards themselves without seeming to try.

Puny words   Some words and phrases can diminish the influence of what you are saying.

Rapport   A deep sense of connection between two people.

Reciprocation   When you give me something in return for something I have given or promised to you.

"Sale-must-end-on-Sunday" principle   We are influenced by the fear of something no longer being available.

"Shock, awe and laughter"   The unexpected can interrupt a pattern of thinking and open us up to influence.

Source effect   The source of information we receive can affect how we evaluate the information.

"Too much choice" effect   Offered too many choices, we are sometimes afraid to make a decision, in case we get it wrong.

"Your-doctor-would-tell-you-to" principle   We are influenced by people who have credibility.

Learn more

Here are six of the best of the many books about influence:

Flipnosis: The Art of Split-second Persuasion by Kevin Dutton (William Heinemann, 2010)

Influence: Science and Practice by Robert B. Cialdini (Pearson Education, 2008)

The Five Paths to Persuasion: The art of selling your message by Robert B. Miller and Gary A Williams, with Alden M. Hayashi (Kogan Page, 2005)

The Science of Influence by Kevin Hogan (John Wiley & Sons, 2005)

Yes! 50 Secrets from the Science of Persuasion by Noah J. Goldstein, Steve J. Martin and Robert B. Cialdini (Profile Books Ltd, 2007)

The Handling Resistance Pocketbook by Mike Clayton (Management Pocketbooks, 2010)

Index